Mercy of God's Humility

Mercy of God's Humility

The *Daily Telegraph* Meditations

Edward Norman

continuum
LONDON • NEW YORK

Continuum
The Tower Building   15 East 26th Street
11 York Road   New York
London SE1 7NX   NY 10010

www.continuumbooks.com

First published 2004

British Library Cataloguing-in-Publication Data
A catalogue record for this book is available from the British Library.

ISBN 0–8264–7128–5 (paperback)

Typeset by RefineCatch Limited, Bungay, Suffolk
Printed and bound by Cromwell Press Ltd, Trowbridge, Wilts

Contents

vii

Introduction

ഇറ

Looking back at the letters I have received, over the last ten years, from readers of the *Meditation* column in the *Daily Telegraph*, two things become immediately clear. The first is an emphatic impression that they are from people who are deeply distressed at the state of the Church in Britain, and who blame its leaders, and not the 'spirit of the age', for its present incoherence and inconsequence. The second is that the writers have themselves given up attendance at church services, finding them no longer familiar or evocative of divine truths, yet are still decisively Christian. In my writings they seem to have discovered a voice which articulates sentiments no longer delivered in their local place of worship, an expression of religious belief in correspondence with the Christianity taught to them when young. Many of the letters are from the elderly. Since I am, I suppose, a 'traditionalist' – at least to the extent that I believe Christianity to be true in the simple sense in which Christ said his message was to be received as by little children – it is hardly surprising that my offerings are well received by others who treasure a faith delivered to them by convinced adherents. Liberalism in religion has always seemed to me to be a temporary phenomenon; an attempt to reinterpret revealed truths according to modern secular dogmas which are themselves so unstable as to elicit everlasting revisionism. There will be no liberals at the end of the world: there will then be nothing left against which to adjust understanding. The truths which Jesus conveyed have, of their nature, to be comprehensible to the great generality of humanity – who have constituted the membership of the Church, and not the thinking classes, since the beginning. If my writings have helped those whose assent to faith suggests the simplicity of children I am grateful, the more so since the concepts I have introduced, and the manner of my writing, have been uncompromisingly academic in tone. I have hoped, however, that this may be distinguished from the configuration of the Faith made by the liberals, whose reinterpretations of Christianity have constructed a religion only capable of being embraced by those immersed in the educated discourse of the middle classes. That so many of my readers are plainly elderly points to an accumulated wisdom in those whose lives have not prepared them for anything like the collapse of institutionalized religion which they see occurring all around them. Their insights pick out the essentials of faith lying in the debris. But there is also a danger here. For there was no golden age of faith; no time when the profession of Christian belief did not involve unceasing controversy and unending battle with what some perceived as an entry of the world into the Church, and others recognized as timely redefinitions of truth.

This last consideration prompts a reflection on the liability of modern Church leaders to avoid controversy. Their vocations sometimes seem dedicated to the pursuit of pragmatism and expediency, to keep the ship afloat without much regard to the principles of sailing. The authors of my letters see this too, and complain about it. The frank name for all the accommodations and 'middle-ground solutions' and forms of words devised in order to disguise authentic divergences of principle, is appeasement. Anglican leaders, in particular, are greatly given to it. But Jesus spoke of his followers as engaged in a conflict, and the gentle worldliness of modern Anglicanism, despite its allure to all the good people who conduct the affairs of the Church of England, seems set in another dimension – light-years away from the searing convictions and singular love of God which led the first fishermen of Galilee to leave their nets and follow him. Institutions are planted in the world and require the arts of the world for their survival; but a Church will inevitably fail if its essential beliefs become secondary. Truth is exact and precise – the revealed truth delivered by God himself when he was in the world has recognizable statements which are the same in all ages and all cultures. Leaders of religious opinion may find it convenient to avoid controversy by rendering them in language so generalized and so imprecise as to attract the assent of virtually all people of goodwill and benign intention: but their restatements are a deception. 'The ungodly have laid a snare for me: but yet I swerved not from thy commandments.' The Lord lived in a context of time, and he addressed himself to the people of time in images appropriate to their understanding. We are called to do the same, for the Church is literally the body of Christ in the world today. It is the expression of the truth, and not the truth itself, which is to be refreshed, however. The feeling is abroad, as my correspondents indicate, that in our own day the treasures are being lost in the sands of revisionism in a manner which has escaped control. The changes are sometimes so profound that both their advocates and their critics lose sight of the essential perspectives from which they were once viewed. Their verbalizing is obstructive; they cannot see the wood for the trees.

Here is an illustration. Christianity is about obligations owed to God, and the observance of the laws he has established for the conduct of individual lives. It is about our *identity* – that we are owned by God and have no other primary loyalties in the world. It is about the worship of God: an offering (not intended to elicit emotional satisfaction or social camaraderie in ourselves) which is directed to the Creator of all things for his own sake. Because humans are flawed, and are defined by the sinfulness of their natures, the profession of religious belief begins with repentance and proceeds thereafter very much against the grain. It hurts; it involves sacrifices of the things we would rather do; the priorities of our lives have to undergo radical change. And even then the new life in Christ does not release us from the baneful effects of our fallen natures: what it does is to give to each person the spiritual status of being forgiven by him. Then begins citizenship in the Kingdom of Heaven, or the first stages of eternal life – a condition which starts now, while the believer is still in the world, still engaged with the sin which encompasses existence, a life born to misery yet touched by the splendour which only they can know who are received in forgiveness by the Saviour. What of the Christianity actually declared in modern pulpits and owned, in vague tones, by the leaders? It is a riot of sentiment, made to depend on the emotional needs or the social consciousness of the individual. As if in crude corre-spondence to the market forces which encourage modern people in selective consumerism, religious belief is presented as a set of choices, from which potential adherents may pick out favourites – for the religion of our day is all about the enhancement of the human person. Here is the consecration of Humanism; religion as therapy. People go to church not in order to make an offering of time to God but for the emotional sensation apparently to be derived. This understanding of religion is centred in the person and in personal needs. It is, in a way, a revival of the popular religiosity of the cults of the ancient world, or of the folk Christianity of medieval Europe, in which votive offerings were made to particular divinities or saints for assistance with the irksome duties of daily life, or for relief from various sorts of human inconvenience – sickness being high on the list of expectations. Much of this neo-paganism is portent-ously acclaimed as concern for human welfare, now redefined as the essence of Christianity. The ethical ideas of the modern world also are not derived from recognizable philosophical systems or revealed truths: they are constructed, on the hoof, by appointed sages on ethical committees intended to advise governmental agencies, and operate on the understated assumption that the ethical may be recognized in whatever appears most conducive to human material welfare. Similarly, the endless hospital dramas served up as nightly entertainment on television screens encourage the sense, to which the public seems only too attentive, that the emotional luxuriance of the ward has replaced the church as the place where human values may be discerned in their finest expression. It is sanctified Humanism; man and his needs has replaced God and his majesty in the centre stage of modern Christian drama. No wonder people write to a newspaper columnist who cheekily attempts to scatter the house of cards. In an age obsessed by humanity and its worth, religion, too, is being interpreted as an emotional adjunct to human self-esteem. The *Meditation* articles, of which a second selection follows, were written to deny that this is an authentic understanding of Christian truth.

As it breaks up upon the rocks, the Church of England now presents a very dispiriting spectacle. Self-absorbed, increasingly limited in its intellectual capacity, directed by those plainly more concerned with managerial enterprise than with the actual saving of souls, it is moving rapidly to the margins of social existence. Many of its senior figures seem preoccupied with protecting themselves from controversy until their retirement age arrives; men of expediency rather than of principle. And they are still mostly *men*, too. Whatever the ecclesiological propriety of the ordination of women to the priesthood, the fact remains that many anticipated a great infusion of new insights and new vitality into the life of the Church of England. It has not happened. There has been a kind of *feminizing* of religion, but this would appear to derive from more general cultural sources than from a distinct contribution by women ministers. Women tend to understand religion as an affair of welfare, caring, and human relationships. Men seem to be more interested in doctrine and ideas. Even to suggest such a distinction – and it is done with full acknowledgement of its imperfection – is to provoke something like outrage. But when women were first ordained we were all assured that they had a *distinct* contribution to make. What, if it was not in the kind of areas I have just indicated, was the exact nature of this contribution? There can be no doubting the existence of an unexpressed disappointment with the result of women's priestly ministry so far: certainly the decline of the Church as an institution has in no discernible degree been decelerated by it.

The clergy in general are very demoralized. They remain, like the whole Church of England, still recognizably middle class in social values and attitudes – though the orientation has adjusted downwards from middle to lower middle class. That, at any rate, should produce some benefits, at least to the extent that it indicates a slight broadening of the base. Unfortunately, however, the actual base itself is now so insubstantial that as the Church implodes its social class characteristics become increasingly irrelevant. When some of those who write to me revisit a church in which they once worshipped they encounter an unfamiliar world. Now the seats are likely to be arranged informally around a central table, and an atmosphere of simulated camaraderie encompasses the proceedings, which are attended by a small company of increasingly unrepresentative people. The introduction of the 'kiss of peace' at Holy Communion – traditionally observed in the Roman Catholic Church through the centuries in a highly ritualized gesture of greeting – has, since the 1970s among Anglicans, become a momentary up-heaval of emotional release (embarrassing to those unfamiliar with such goings-on) which actually demonstrates how un-inclusive the Church is becoming. Probably nothing has put people off going to church more than this extraordinary piece of quasi-liturgical theatre. The new service books compound the problem of seeking forms of worship which attempt simul-taneously to satisfy individual preferences and yet to be general enough to convey the impression of a united body. The old *Book of Common Prayer* was the major shared inheritance which kept the Church of England together. After decades of experimentation, in which the congregations were removed further and further from uniformity, the new books called *Common Worship* have finally abandoned the concept of a single manner of addressing God. Worship committees in each parish select among a huge number of alternative forms, and daily and seasonal changes in the services themselves operate to stimulate variety and individualism in worship. It is impos-sible to build a spiritual life around the shifting permutations – as traditionally was possible with the old *Book of Common Prayer*, whose collects and readings shaped each year with familiar markers of spiritual formation. Having ransacked its own liturgical inheritance, the Church of England has replaced it with services which are trite, banal, and occasionally lapse into actual grammatical error. It is difficult to see what has been gained. In hindsight it is now possible to realize that the old *Book of Common Prayer* should have been edited for modern usage and put into decent modern English: opening the Pando-ra's box of liturgical change may have satisfied the liturgical ennui of the professional liturgists, but worshippers have left the churches in droves.

It is also now difficult to determine the nature of party allegiances in the Church, especially for those accustomed to characterizing them in terms of High, Liberal and Evangelical. The High Church seems shell-shocked after so many changes, especially in relation to the ministry of women. The Liberals are where they have always been – seeking to accommodate the secular moral seriousness of the age. But the Evangelicals are problematical. Having digested, and so killed off, the old Low

Church, they are now the most influential section in the Church: as witness all the refrains and spiritual ejaculations in the new service books. They are, however, internally incoherent, some tending to an unexpected penchant for ritual, others achieving an absorption with issues-based agendas of the sort previously associated with the Liberal wing. Perhaps the most apposite manner of categorizing the Evangelicals is by dividing Anglicans between those who believe they have received personal experience of the divine presence, and those whose authority for their beliefs derives from integration with the historic witness of the institutional Church. This definition would leave out the Liberals, but liberalism in religion does not need a *religious* authority since its ideals are anyway procured from the texture of secular opinion. These distinctions are also messy, since virtually all the matters which come before the synods are liable to divide Anglicans in yet more novel ways. Once individualism in religion has taken root, as it has in Britain and the Western world generally, private judgement becomes sovereign in all areas of debate, and the essential reference to which people resort for the authority of their judgements becomes quite arbitrary. Some select a recent television documentary, others attend to a moralistic urge conceived in response to an item in the news. All imagine their chosen course of action and belief to be a modern representation of Gospel truths. As the features of the Church of England set gently into those of a cadaver, the last hold on life appears to be a grasp for the politically correct. Perhaps the most satisfactory way of describing the division within modern Christianity is in terms of contrast between those who believe it to be true in the sense received through the centuries, and those who consider it to be a texture of sacred myths whose divine content is inexplicit and general.

The Church has ceased to be incorporated with the intelligentsia, and now gleans its values as outsiders. In no other area is its marginalization proving to be so damaging to its prophetic function. The intellectual quality of the bishops is considered less important than their managerial skills, and the levels of education achieved by those coming forward for ordination have fallen a long way beneath those acceptable in the professions generally. On the face of it the large network of Church schools should secure a continued Christian presence in education; the reality, however, is that very many of these schools are in practice conducted according to the same secular principles as the educational system around them. The Church has lost any serious presence in higher education, being represented by pastoral chaplains – whose pastoral advice tends strongly to avoid any suggestion of distinctly Christian doctrinal or moral content – and by liberal scholars unable or unwilling to promote Christianity in any recognizably institutional sense. The Church of England has seen its control of higher education dismantled in the last two centuries yet has done nothing to create a Christian university of its own – as has happened in many other countries. It lives on, just about, apparently unaware that it lives on borrowed time. Excluded from an effective educational presence, it sees its mission as most effectively conveyed through pastoral work. 'See how they beg for a piece of spirit', as Nietzsche said, 'when they are denied a piece of meat.'

Many of those who write to me are puzzled that the Church does not 'speak out' more clearly on moral issues. By this they usually mean questions of sexual morality. It has to be said that on matters of social and economic morality the Church of England has a lengthy record, and on the whole a baneful one. In my BBC Reith Lectures in 1978, I attempted to show how in the frequent pronouncements then being made by the General Synod there was a very close correspondence between the principles endorsed by the Church and the liberal ideals of the secular movers of opinion. Now that has nearly all passed away. The criticisms of 'power structures' and capitalism, and the undisguised support of advanced trades union claims and of revolutionary movements in the developing world, have left little trace, and are, indeed, now discerned through a glass darkly, period-pieces of an aborted radicalism. When my letter writers refer to morals they mean sexual conduct. They are untroubled about questions of political science: whether the Church of England, even though technically still the national Establishment of religion, should any longer address the whole society on its moral conduct, in view of the claims increasingly insisted upon, that this is now a society of plural values. They do see, as I do, that the Church has an obligation to inform its own members on principles and conduct of sexual morality. The difficulty is they notice, as I do also, that the range of opinion on these issues inside the Church exactly parallels that outside, and that opinions are not derived from the Church's own treasury of moral theology but from the same areas of journalism and television debate as inform society at large. Having picked up random moral ideas in this way Christians, both leaders and those in the pews, then attempt to reinterpret scriptural teaching to endorse them. The resulting rag-bag of attitudes shows a distinct departure, on many issues, from the principles declared by the Church over the centuries. Those who write to me are not in general concerned with the authentically new areas of knowledge, as in the determination of Christian teaching on, for example, gene selection processes or stem-cell research, but are simply worried – outraged would perhaps express it more accurately – that the bishops and clergy do not condemn adultery, divorce, and various sorts of conduct which they have been accustomed to regard as perversions. There are, of course, some generational problems here. The substance of their criticisms, however, is in most things well-placed. Particularly on matters like the re-marriage of the divorced, or homosexuality, they cannot understand why centuries of very clear teaching are being abandoned. The truth is in fact very simple. The bishops and clergy are terrified of offending 'enlightened opinion', or of transgressing the canons of political correctness. Their moral cowardice, however, may at least be excused over just those issues where genuinely new insights into human sexuality may inform revision of received traditional moral precepts – I believe myself that homosexuality falls into this category – and where all *truth* should be recognized as of God. There can be no excuse, surely in any circumstances, for the tacit acceptance of 'partnerships' in place of Christian marriage, acceptance of abortion, or a more or less complete failure to address the evils consequent upon the sexualization of popular culture. With increasingly little to say about its theological claims, the Church speaks with ever more stumbling lips on basic matters of sexual conduct. Yet sexual relationships are the most commonplace form in which most Christians are confronted with moral choice, and they are entitled to clear teaching from the institutional Church. Unhappily, another generational division opens up. Christian adherents who are young or middle-aged often reject the right of the Church leaders to determine their moral attitudes, and believe themselves capable of devising their own judgements in such matters. We are back, once again, at the eclectic spirituality of our day – of religion interpreted as an affair of individual spirituality. Here may be recognized the inheritance of decades, now, in which schoolchildren are encouraged to regard all religious ideas as of equal validity. 'They will not be learned nor understand, but walk on still in darkness; all the foundations of the earth are out of course.'

Yet even in its broken fragments there is still something lovely about the Church of England, its noble aspirations and its record of declaring Christian truths somehow undiminished by the fearful catastrophe that has overtaken it in our day. Perhaps it never really was a 'branch' of the universal Church, and is now only a fading memory of past conflicts, a severed limb whose living fluids have drained away. Yet the hopes of many saintly men and women have found a refuge in her foliage, and there are still many of us who are grateful for the home we have found in her shadow. The *Daily Telegraph* is the last national newspaper to print a regular column explicitly intended to uphold Christian belief, and, as these paragraphs have shown, those who write to express their opinions or their gratitude are taken extremely seriously. There is an authentic ministry here; a chance to offer both teaching and consolation. And encouragement: for as St Paul knew so well, in the evanescent letters that he sent to those who were often confused or dispirited, Christians have a primary duty to encourage one another.

One

Watching space

ঙ৩ও

It is often supposed that the seeds of intellectual doubt about the truth of Christianity were sown in the nineteenth century by a perceived conflict of science and religion. Its centre was the debate about evolution: but even then, in fact, discerning minds recognized that no such inherent conflict really existed. Intellectual scepticism was accelerated in the last century, however, and its agents were the anthropologists and the archaeologists. What they discovered was the commonplace nature of the Jewish experience. Revealed religion had depended on the uniqueness of Israel: a people chosen by God, guided through sequences of formative religious education, delivered in a divine act of cosmic salvation, and specially endowed with territory. The realization in the nineteenth century that the Jewish people were in fact just like other ancient peoples – recovering from the trauma of conquest, and formed through a folk-wandering in pursuit of a land to settle – produced an horrific frisson amongst orthodox believers. For it relativized the historic foundations of faith, and, for many educated interpreters, cast destructive doubt upon the significance of the Jewish revelation.

In the twentieth century exactly the same thing is happening, but on a hugely enlarged scale. Now it is the human race itself which is losing its unique significance, partly because knowledge of other forms of life on earth is creating an understanding of mankind which leaves him inseparable from the general living mass, and partly because of what may usefully be called space culture. It is this second which has a popular basis and is therefore, in the era of universal education, the more insidious.

Discoveries about the unimaginable extent of the universe cast doubt upon the unique nature of human life: life on this tiny speck may have no significance nor be especially remarkable. There is an enormous popular belief that 'aliens' observe the earth from their space vehicles, or that hugely intelligent 'beings' elsewhere in the universe may eventually communicate – or worse, visit. A lot of this is simply silly fantasy; elements of it may in some sense be true. But anyone who doubts the pervasiveness of the space culture should look at television cartoons made for children, or refer to the statistics of those who believe in the existence of flying saucers. The psychology in all this is not new, however. Much of popular space culture has a strong magical dimension – thinly disguised as superior technology. And the experience of those who think they have been abducted by aliens is precisely that of all those medieval neurotics who believed they had been violated by demons. Let no one ignore the straws in the wind: the burgeoning space culture of our day is diminishing the significance of human life in a manner that assails the centre of Christian understanding. This is that God raised humanity above the rest of the Creation, and revealed himself as involved with its destiny. He may have revealed himself comparably to other worlds, too, but the space culture of our day is a fictional not a sure base for supposing that.

Two

All Saints

೮ා౦ෂ

It is All Saints Day today. And who is a saint? The complexity of our natures makes none of us simply good or simply bad: we are the consequences of too many conditions over which we have no control. Each person is formed by genetic determination, infant experience, and acquired ideas. The disposition to structured behaviour finds its expression in an enormous number of alternatives, and the definition of goodness or badness attached to particular modes of behaviour shows a high degree of relative judgement through time and culture. In one age a man is accounted good, for example, because he seeks the punishment of those who spread opinions regarded as erroneous or vicious by the prevailing culture; in another he is condemned for lack of liberalism or tolerance. We are determined in so many ways, and our minds are opened to alternatives in such an arbitrary and piecemeal fashion, that it must sometimes seem hopeless to try to isolate definitions of authentic goodness. Modern knowledge has exposed the nuts and bolts of the human psyche; the decay of an agreed basis for ethic value has robbed us of certainties about the estimates we should make of our own conduct.

But sanctity is not actually about goodness – at least in the ordinary sense society now understands. The saint is the one who tries to transcend his nature, or to use its ambiguous directives for spiritual formation. Thus sanctity begins with self-awareness, and in a universally fallen creation that means awareness of sin. That is why the teaching of Jesus began with a call to repentance. No one can be recognized as a Christian, least of all a saint, who does not regularly confess sin and ask for forgiveness. While in the world, however, we continue to be conditioned by our natures, and the attempts at sanctity – at transcending our circumstance – will be partial. Saints may be people who are not capable of overall goodness, but whose lives in one or more dimensions of spirituality achieve insight and expression. To the eyes of the world they may seem unpromising candidates for holiness. Jesus was censured in his day for consorting with sinners, some of whom, in responding to his call, became truly saints. Doubtless in many things their lives remained unreconstructed, and to the conventional their spiritual aspirations must have seemed negligible. But not to God. It still shocks people today to be told that Jesus loves child molesters and murderers; and criminals may even achieve sanctity if in other dimensions of their nature they seek submission to the will of God and amend their lives. Those whom the Lord calls to spiritual awareness are not transformed in the whole of their humanity. The corruption in their natures endures; it is their attempts at personal transcendence which furnish the materials of the spiritual life. Who is a saint? Saints are people like us, people who try to see God. Any simple goodness we acquire in the process is merely a by-product.

Three

Death wish

ಬಿ‍ಿಆ

A person's attitude to death relates a great deal about how he sees life. It is actually very instructive that when someone is asked for their response to the death of a well-known public figure their reply inevitably conveys the state of their feelings rather than an evaluation of the unfortunate deceased. Thus the first reaction is not 'he was a very great man', or whatever, but 'I was shocked', or 'I felt devastated'. Death is in this sense an indicator of egocentricity: the value of life is measured by the extent to which it affects our personal emotions. The death of a celebrity, therefore, becomes the occasion for excessive self-dramatizing, an indulgence which is perhaps harmless enough in itself but which encourages a kind of pseudo-reality in which the self is made the arbiter of all things. The control of grief is like the pursuit of happiness, or any other human emotional impulsion: its indulgence is bad for spiritual health. It is also true that dramatizing death allows a market for the manufacture of myth. So often the qualities that are attributed to a person at death were not really possessed by them but are simply conventional pieties of the age. This, too, is probably harmless in itself, but is an offence against truth. It also operates both ways. Celebrities or public figures create a propaganda image for public consumption in their lifetime, and if observers choose to take that at face value, and to enhance it with the mystique of death, so be it. The history of human society is full of fairly worthless people who achieved fame by such means – these days some are assisted by expensive professional consultants. Yet it is as well to remember that those accounted corrupt or evil at the time of their demise may actually have been possessed of spiritual or personal qualities which the world's consensus did not see. The greater the integrity of a person the less likely it is that they will parade their qualities to achieve recognition in their lifetime. It was the man who went into the Temple to pray and who confessed himself a sinner, rather than the virtuous man who declaimed his virtue, who was commended by Christ.

Death should be the occasion of remembering that we are all in the end very similar – given to human failings, limited by our natures, sometimes striving for self-improvement, always ambiguous in our motives. It used to be the great virtue of the Anglican Funeral Service that it was the same for everyone; the cool words of the Prayer Book reminding us of the wretchedness of human achievement and the supervening mercy of God. Today, characteristically, mourners like to personalize funerals, using the service as an occasion to eulogize their loved ones, and expunging, as far as they are able, mention of death itself. And so they are robbed of a most significant moment to set existence into a realistic context. We are given life as a gift; we leave the earth with an added value that is known only to God.

Four

The false dawn

ᨁᨁ

In former ages men and women had a fear of the unknown. Their lives were passed in a world which seemed to be subject to mysterious forces of good and evil, where natural events portended the will of gods and demons, where sickness and mental disorder were personal afflictions sent as punishments or warnings, where dreams were prophetic, and where, when night fell, the darkness released unspeakable terrors. In the pagan religions the lives of individuals were at the mercy of arbitrary divinities, and even in Christianized cultures surviving superstition, and an imperfect cosmology, held people in dreadful thrall. Human ills were accepted with fatalism, and such remedies as were available for personal or social misfortune were often applied in ignorance of their baneful side-effects. Enlightenment came gradually, and in general with the support of Christianity – it is largely a myth of nineteenth-century secularists (citing the unusual case of Galileo) that the Church was opposed to scientific investigation of the world and its phenomena. The Church had inherited and encouraged the cosmic speculations of Antiquity, and it was in its educational institutions that the seeds of modern science began to germinate. Modern Islamic learning shows how readily a vigorously religious view of humanity can be compatible with basic acceptance of a scientific world-view.

But enlightenment did not produce emancipation. Men and women released from fear of the dark forces of an ignorant understanding of the world placed themselves in subjection to a new captivity of the human spirit. Fear of the unknown has been replaced by fear of the known. People today, for example, are terrified of cancer to a degree equal to, and perhaps even in excess of, their former fear of illness as an agent of providential fate. Once their religious teachers informed them with stark messages about the impending end of the world; today people are just as worried because they know about the probable means of that catastrophe – a nuclear exchange, a new virus, or the toxic effects of the planet itself colliding with space debris being the favoured candidates. Our unreasonable expectations to freedom from unhappiness, to secure relationships, to satisfying work, to a comfortable old age, are all or in part unattainable. The world mockingly reminds us that, for all our knowledge and scientific capability, we are not actually in control of our destiny. We are like Canute at the water's edge, forever willing a mastery of events which we shall never possess.

The life of mankind remains visited by fears, and despite our medical expertise and our social engineering, it is as frail as ever. If we would recover wisdom we should return to the description of humanity given in the Bible, and seek to combine our emancipation from eradicable worldly suffering with a renewed acceptance of our personal imperfection. It is God who is in control.

Five

Changing times

ৰ৴৻য়

There is widespread consciousness of the decline of religious belief and observance in Western societies; Pope John Paul II spoke of it at the time of the Paris rally for young people in August of this year. What is less noticed is the extent to which the Christian recession is not leaving a void but is being replaced by something else. The difficulty is that the replacement does not have a name by which it can be identified, neither does it have a systematic basis or a coherent statement of its principles. It is a collection of moral declamations. It is centred not on God but on humanity and its needs. Christianity is about the sovereignty of God and obedience owed to him; its replacement is about the welfare of men and women. Christianity makes demands about individual spiritual formation and the requirement of a disciplined life; its replacement is hedonistic, allowing all kinds of licence in the 'private' lives of individuals but imposing strict moral attitudes in social and welfare issues. Christianity is about forgiveness; its replacement seeks the punishment and correction of those who offend against right conduct. Christianity is, or ought to be, dogmatic – it rests upon precise statements of belief, and because the Church is the body of Christ in the world it needs to be very exacting in what is declared in his name. It is the voice of Christ himself who speaks through his earthly representatives. Its replacement, in another contrast, is not greatly exercised about ultimate beliefs, but puts the material well-being of men and women above religious convictions.

This emerging religion of secular Humanism, which is often popularly identified as applied Christianity, but is actually applied materialism, is producing its own saints. These are people of acknowledged moral virtue, not in their private lives – which are often accepted as being messy – but in their concern for the afflicted or in their devotion to good causes. They are the role model of the carers, and their sanctification most typically occurs in the wards of hospitals or in the stations of the emergency services. These are places, incidentally, which are glamorized and sentimentalized in television entertainment series, and fulfil the sort of heroic function which the mission field and the monastic cloister once provided in the lives of authentic saints. Much good undoubtedly derives from the succour encouraged by the religion of humanity. Its dark side, however, is its ignorance of the dark side of humanity itself, its impatience with ideological formulations, its appeal to false expectations about the capacity for human improvement, and its evocation of a species of moral tyranny – it is extremely intolerant of unbelievers and of its own heretics. It is also, in general, unforgiving.

Christianity, on the other hand, is addressed to sinners. Christ did not, on his own testimony, come for the righteous, and of the conventionally good he observed simply that they had their reward. Jesus is the Saviour of the morally inadequate, of the impure, of those who can't cope, of child molesters and rapists, of the uncertain, of those who know what they ought to do but somehow don't have the strength to do it. His hand of pity is extended to such as these, as well as to the moral and correct people – who, if anything, will not feel the need to reach out and grasp it.

Six

The price of salvation

&❍&

One of the things which modern people are unprepared to accept about religious belief is that it shall cost them anything in personal terms. They are, that is to say, more interested in religion as a 'beautiful' dimension, as an assistance in times of difficulty, than they are in the notion of observance – that religion makes demands on our conduct and on the management of our lives. We live in an age of welfare entitlements and human rights, and there is a tendency for religion to get lumped together with all the other benefits as a kind of enrichment of lifestyle. Like aesthetic sensation or successful emotional relationships, it is perceived as pleasurable and as imparting significance to the individual. That religious belief involves self-denial, the surrender of worldly options, submission to divine sovereignty, moral discipline, and abstinence, is not on most people's agenda. Religion, for so many, is merely the sanctification of existing modes of living, a type of therapy, a sentimental attachment to a warm appraisal of human worth. The religion of Jesus began with a call to personal repentance, and a conviction in the individual that God invites a radical reconstruction of what we are. The Christianity of modern Western people, in contrast, is not expected to result in either a major change of personal circumstance or a revolution in social attitudes. Indeed, the prevalent moralism of the times is in practice secular: the welfare culture may or may not have religious resonance for those who are its enthusiasts. The welfare culture is a version of Humanism, and to that extent is an unconscious implementation of a materialist view of mankind. Its vision is restricted to the world, and it recognizes no sovereign outside of human need. Caring has replaced prayer as the spring of moral consciousness.

A call to authentic religion will involve a call to privation. Few of us are strong enough to be very effective in this, and the comfortable acceptance of a relatively painless lifestyle which is marked by no salient heights or depths of goodness or corruption describes the condition of most of us. But Jesus called men and women to give up even family loyalties for his sake; to follow him into the desert places – symbolic representations of the life of sacrifice, in which the familiar props are discarded and the stark facts of our natures are exposed. Modern people are fairly uncritical about human nature, and have in general a generous estimate of human worth. The qualities of humanity depicted in the Bible are very different; there we are seen as creatures in rebellion against God. The mystery of religion is that God is involved with us at all. To observe men and women is not to see very promising material for those who are actually, in God's mercy, called to creative work. For God transcends our comprehension, and the fact that Jesus offers us salvation, despite the horrific things we do, is taken quite casually by us – as though it was a kind of entitlement. Such is the nature of human pride.

Seven

_____

Christmas

ଚ୍ଚ)ଓଃ

Consider the enormous contrast between the creative power of God and the natures of men and women. The more we learn about the expanse and complexity of the universe, the more awesome it all seems: countless forms of matter, some of terrifying strangeness. Our world itself no longer seems to be the centre of all things but a tiny speck in a tiny part of the vastness of space. It is a measure of the secularization of intellectual culture that this unfolding understanding of Creation, instead of adding to a sense of the greatness of God, merely induces scepticism about his existence at all. The real danger is that God will no longer be recognized as a person, with attributes of which ours are an imperfect copy, but as some kind of creative impulse or first cause. The primitive religions of the world, indeed, conceived God in just such a manner – an earth divinity whose spirit resided in elements of nature. Christmas is about the action of a personal God, who came into the world in a demonstration of his relationship with his own creation. Humanity had before that known about God through witnessing his power in the natural order, and because God had also chosen to reveal himself through historical events and evolving cultures. Progressively men and women came to see that the God who was known in this way was not some elemental spirit but a person; and when God actually came into the world as flesh he was able to convey precise knowledge about himself and his laws by confirming the images people had come to use to describe the spiritual presence, and to consecrate by his shared humanity the value of existence itself. Increasingly, in the present moment of Western culture, Christmas is being re-interpreted as a celebration of warm *human* qualities. It is fast becoming a time to mark up the virtues of caring and welfare. The real message of Christmas, however, transcends such necessary but commonplace preoccupations: it is about the great love of God, not the transient cares of humanity.

For the miracle of Christmas is that the author of all things – of the astonishing universe – chose to involve himself with the creatures his creative power had enabled to generate upon this otherwise obscure planet. When we contemplate the dreadful facts of human nature and conduct the marvel is all the greater. People are called by God to assist in the creative process, to develop the earth, and to share divine knowledge by using its resources, and to reflect upon their own fate and circumstance. People are capable of goodness and altruism. But they are also corrupted at the very centre of their beings, self-seeking, emotionally indulgent, lacking in judgement, given to wrong choices, and selfish. How is it possible to believe in a God of such august power yet who cares for the least esteemed in human society? The answer lay in the manger at Bethlehem, the God who became man, who suffered for our sakes, and who now calls us to surrender our worldly priorities and to follow him.

Eight

———

At the year's end

৪০০৪

In the dying days of a year people's thoughts often touch upon the significance of time itself. Another year passes, and its events, both public and personal, descend to the sediment of accumulating memory, sometimes with regret, occasionally with relief. It is as well to remember that God himself works through time, and that our consciousness of his presence in the perpetual sequences of temporal change is important in our response to the purposes of existence. God works through time in the sense that the Creation was a definable event: it did not occur through some gradual coincidence of influences, for all our modern knowledge seems to indicate a single and dramatic happening. The universe began and expanded, and persists in expansion, and time is the indicator of its progress. Now the Bible, and the words of Christ himself, are clear that the end, comparably, will be a single event. By 'end' is meant human life, reality as understood in relation to human habitation of the earth. Scriptural teaching also indicates that this will be some shocking cataclysm, perhaps like the one which ended the occupation of the world by the dinosaurs. Then the planet seems to have been coated with the debris of a collision with material from space. The earth itself endured, with some of its life-forms, but was regenerated in a different mode, with us as a consequence. God can make all things new. The end of the world – our world – may not therefore be the end of the planet as such, but only the end of the human race. 'In those days', Christ is recorded as saying, in St Mark's Gospel, 'the sun shall be darkened, and the moon shall not give her light; and the stars of heaven shall fall.' The dreadful day which witnessed the

———
15

demise of the dinosaurs must have been just such a time; and time, or the movement of materials in space, may yet, in the divine scheme, provide the occasion for the last account of humanity. Christians should live their lives as if that moment is imminent.

Taking stock of time is thus a Christian imperative. It enables a daily audit of our personal use of time – whether we have been profligate with such a precious commodity, or whether we have expended enough of it in the service of God's purposes. It is a strange paradox that in an age like ours, when men and women seek to prolong life, there is less and less awareness of any serious purpose to it. Individual lives have become a pursuit of security and happiness; time is an irritating impediment, an unwelcome reminder of personal decay. Christians are those who perceive an extremely serious purpose both to life and to time. It is nothing less than spiritual formation, converting the ingredients of life into the durable substance of participation with providence, to deploy qualities which have about them the materials of eternity. This goes against many of the common assumptions of humanity, for it is to deny the world's priorities and to reach out into the unfathomable purposes of God.

Nine

The end of life

❧☙

For many people life is a nexus of injustices. At the simplest level, their motives are misunderstood or misrepresented by others, or the good they try to do somehow rebounds and produces negative consequences. In another remove, their lives are marked by opportunities which ought to have opened up but did not, or their talents and hard work go unrewarded when others seem to forge ahead in the stakes of worldly success. Children show ingratitude after years dedicated to their upbringing; marriage partners, or partners, desert, or perhaps cruellest of all, a lifelong search for someone to love proves barren. It is possible, indeed it is common, that after years of providing for security some upheaval of the market, or whatever, robs people of their protection in old age. Sickness has a very random incidence, and people today are convinced that health is a kind of entitlement: they are wrong in this but their feeling is real enough as a cause of a sense of injustice. Death itself, particularly when it visits a partner or a close family relation, is railed against in a society which does not know how to cope with it. Above all, as time delivers us into old age, life as a whole can be seen to have been a disappointment, an assemblage of unfulfilled ambitions and unrecognized effort.

These are all, however, attitudes of our own contrivance. We do not need to feel injustice. In objective terms our treatment at the hands of fate, or of others, is certainly often unfair – but we are people, not objects, and it is *our* choice when we estimate the world as a catalogue of the benefits which will fall to us. Of course less worthy people than ourselves flourish – less worthy in our own definition, and perhaps really so by some absolute standard. One certain thing is that it is not the virtuous but self-publicists and the well-connected who inherit the earth. So what? The earth may not be particularly well managed in their custody, but the worth of the individual who beholds it is not affected. The truth is that life does not owe us anything except the chance to use our time in the cultivation of spiritual consciousness. And in that task, as the teaching of Jesus makes clear in, for example, the Sermon on the Mount, there is a kind of reversal of conventional expectations. It is the marginated and the insignificant who achieve authentic insight, and the successful and powerful who are left with little but success and power. The essential part of us, the part of us which is to survive, that is to say, has no worldly tests by which it is recognized: it is the part which has the quality called 'eternal'. Eternal life starts in life; it is life used productively in the individual work of spiritual formation. If our expectations are determined by a desire for worldly recognition, or happiness, or security, or release from pain, then we shall be disappointed. If they are fixed by our determination to glimpse the evidences of the unseen world in the debris of our human hopes they have a realistic chance of delivering us into an eternal life which extends far beyond our experience of earthly society. 'Come to me, all you who labour', Jesus said, 'and I will give you rest.'

Ten

The Resurrection
of Christ

ಬಂಡ

Public opinion polls appear to show that more people believe in personal reincarnation than in the Resurrection of Jesus, and that very many people claim to believe in both. It is not a very encouraging finding. Nor is the growing tendency among Christians to interpret the Resurrection as a symbolical rather than an actual event: that the followers of Jesus sensed his spirit among them, and that their subjective joy comprised a kind of renewal of his life. The simple truth is that the Resurrection is inseparable from the Incarnation itself; it is an affirmation of the nature of the Creation. God does not work by magic, but in the laws of the very matter he has himself exploded into existence and for a while holds in an expanding balance – the universe. To be known about he must either be discovered in the created order itself, by the use of human reason, or he must be evident to our understanding in the only way which is not incompatible with those same laws of Creation: by becoming one of us. Both means of knowing God are available to us. In every culture on the planet men and women have perceived the evidences of a Creator, and have employed their capacity to reason to put their sense that this is so into formal images of God, sometimes, alas, in grotesque ways. God, for his part, entered the immediate experience of humanity by taking upon himself the shared life of his creatures: a supreme act of Revelation which confirmed the preceding intimations of his presence and also directly opened the way of personal salvation to those whose response recognized and acted on his mercy.

It is essential to this divine initiative that God really was a man, and not either the mere *appearance* of a man (as some early heresies taught), or an actual human whom God 'adopted' as his earthly representation (a notion which crops up periodically in each century). Jesus was truly God and truly man. And here is a great paradox; for this was not a 'miraculous' occurence, except according to a very careful definition of the word – modern people tend to use the concept of the miraculous as a kind of synonym for magic. It was an occurrence which fully used the material nature of the Creation, thereby confirming that all God had made was a dimension of his purpose. Now, resurrection stories were attached to numerous local divinities in the cults and mysteries of the ancient world, and were a familiar part of the expectations of those seeking religious help. Such cultic myths were full of bizarre and extraordinary miracles performed by the resuscitated leader. The Resurrection of Christ showed none of these excesses. Instead he returned to the Father; his earthly body, being fully God as well as fully man, ascending (or translating) with the entire power of the author of all things. It was an event both spiritual and material, a unique occurrence which signalled to the children of God – to all people, that is to say – that human life had been endowed with the dignity and purpose of eternal value. Whatever the dreadful imperfections of humanity, the man who is God beckons each one of us to follow him.

Eleven

A discipline for the soul

ဆု©ဆ

It is sometimes noticed, and correctly, that support for religion in traditional societies had an element of entertainment. People went to church because there were few alternative leisure opportunities, and they derived a measure of recreational satisfaction from the social association. The popularity of revivalist preaching is perhaps explained in part by its vivacity and drama. Particularly in rural areas, the Sunday gathering in church provided an exchange of news and a means of becoming acquainted with a wider world. The point should not be laboured, however, principally because attendances at church were not enormous. At the end of the eighteenth century, for example, fewer than fifteen per cent of the population attended the services of the Established Church, and perhaps a nearly equal number resorted to Dissenting chapels. Even the Victorian religious boom, which was largely confined to the middle class, did not dramatically alter these levels of support for formal religion. The new churches then built remained unfilled. They represented the enthusiasm of the moralists rather than any inclination of the working classes to attend. But the element of entertainment was always significant. In a society of limited mobility, few educational opportunities, and low social expectation, the local church was often the place which provided some measure of relief from the travails of the workplace or the family. That society has long been buried, and a television aerial covers its grave.

The trouble is that modern people still expect religion to provide a kind of entertainment. There has been a secularization of the emotions – which are now routinely indulged for reasons which are emancipated from human moral seriousness. Each evening, before the screen, people's emotions move rapidly through a succession of manipulations quite unlike anything experienced in human society before. Like an addictive drug, furthermore, men and women now expect the same levels of emotional satisfaction from real life – and, where they think about it, from religion. Christianity is actually about submission to demands made by God, a surrender to a Sovereign outside our needs. Modern people, however, expect religion, instead, to provide immediate emotional satisfaction. For them it is thought to be a beautiful experience, a sense of interior peace, an aesthetically elevating sensation, a warm encounter with others, a dimension of the universal praise of 'caring'. In each of these facets, and in others, religion today is subordinated to individual emotional gratification; far from representing a consciousness of the terrible majesty of God, religion is becoming a mere accompaniment to personal expectations of emotional reassurance. It is high-minded entertainment. People choose their version of religion according to its capacity to satisfy their needs: the idea that their needs require any kind of discipline does not appeal. Each of us should be reminded every day that God's will and our perception of our own needs do not necessarily coincide.

Twelve

A love that hurts

❧❧

It is right that Christianity should be presented in a way that is immediately accessible, for it was declared by Jesus himself to the humble and to the simple. It is right that anyone should be able to walk into a church and feel at ease with the worship there – the praise offered to God should never be so complicated that specialist intellectual gifts or liturgical knowledge are required to understand it. Accessibility is one thing, however, and reductionism is quite another. Christians today have a tendency to make the faith too *easy*. The way of the Cross exemplified by Christ is hard and demanding; we try to domesticate it within the existing habits of our lives, and, worse, we sometimes try to employ religion as a species of self-gratification. For loving Jesus is about denying ourselves some things which we would otherwise crave, and it is also about taking on obligations which we might otherwise neglect. Christianity, that is to say, is about what we should do for God, not what we expect him to do for us. Of course, God *will* actually help us – as he did in the old Covenant with Israel which spelled out the nature of his concern for his people. But the gifts we receive are by acts of grace; they are not our entitlements. Modern people are now conditioned to regard themselves as possessed, by right, of so many benefits that they readily attach religious consolation to the list. We judge ourselves unfairly treated unless we receive welfare and security, stable human relationships, personal fulfilment – and numerous other attributes of the good life. Christianity, in contrast, is not essentially about our satisfaction, and it is not an agent of therapy, a means of individual significance or happiness. It is a nexus of obligations, the love of God expressed in love of neighbour.

At the very beginning of the way of the Cross, for those who would follow it, stands the dreadful fact of human sin – our sin. At the end is judgement – God's judgement of our use of the life he has entrusted to us. The gate is narrow and the way is hard: and the way starts its course as we recognize the full horror of our sinfulness and seek forgiveness. The trouble is that people don't feel very sinful. They feel, indeed, rather aggrieved, seeing life as a succession of benefits they are somehow owed and which are persistently not delivered. They find it difficult to believe in a God who does not gratify their own evaluation of their worth. Neither do people today want to believe in judgement. It is a discriminatory concept, and discrimination between people is alien to our culture, which is now, for good reason, steeped in objection to discrimination on the basis of race, or class, or sex, or religion. The notion that God, at the end of time, will condemn those who have not made good use of the life he has given them does not have much appeal, and most people appear to be unconscious universalists. 'Provided you are caring you are saved', we seem to be saying. Christ, however, really calls us to a love that is more demanding than that; his love, for his part, is that he bothers at all with a people who are so undeserving.

Thirteen

A morality for all seasons

୫ଠ୧ଓ

It is sometimes said that the private life and moral behaviour of a man or woman has no relevance in judging their fitness for public office. Yet it is difficult to see how such a view can be held. The issue is one of integrity. A person who is unreliable in one dimension of their life is likely to be so in others. It is notably true of public figures that those who are very active in one area of their conduct are likely to be so in all of them – as evidenced, particularly, in sexual behaviour. But the principal unreality about maintaining what some see as a 'liberal' attitude to fitness for office is the separation of 'private' from 'public' moral conduct. We would regard a person who entertains racist opinions as unsuited; why, then, should we think someone who has an unconventional record in sexual relationships any different? Both rest on social acceptability, and most people still regard sexual promiscuity as an unsatisfactory basis for reliability. But there is a sliding-scale of acceptability. We would apparently eliminate child molesters from public office but not serial adulterers. Why do we think the second acceptable behaviour? That can only be a *moral* judgement. If moral approval is to be attached to *any* species of conduct, as surely it unavoidably must, then what kind of religious or philosophical basis do we employ as our standard of judgement? Christians are actually the first to recognize the fact of human moral frailty, and that people of tried ethical goodness may nevertheless lapse at some stage or other into wrong behaviour. That does not make them wrong people, or hypocrites: they are simply people who have human characteristics, including moral fallibility. They would be foolish indeed who rejected the value of an ethical standard on the grounds that it could not always be met.

So the wise course is probably to recognize two sorts of behaviour for those in public office. The first is described by those who believe in an unstructured code of personal behaviour, or who are arbitrary and selective in applying moral norms. Such people are likely to be unsuited to office in a polity which respects ethical consistency. The second comprises those who try to live a moral life but fail. There is a Christian view about such as these, and it encourages a realistic acceptance of human weakness and a reluctance to condemn the whole person through a failing in one part of their being. Most in public life, happily, are probably in this category. But why restrict the matter to *public* life? Each of us is caught up in a nexus of relationships, and people depend on our moral reliability. And for each of us, also, our behaviour in one dimension of our lives is likely to be replicated in all dimensions. It is one of the fearful characteristics of sin that we always see ourselves as an exception when we venture into sinfulness – as if the moral laws somehow do not apply in our personal situation. Be thankful that the Christian God really does love sinners.

Fourteen

Gifts of the Spirit

ॐ

In middle and later years very many people experience a sense of disappointment, or perhaps frustration, that the experience and expertise they have accumulated in life remain substantially unused. This is as true of those in the ordinary circumstances of managing a home, for example, or of work in 'routine' employment, as it is of the specially talented. Years of building up knowledge and vocational wisdom seem to have been for nothing; the world just does not seem to have a place for the gifts which have been so carefully cultivated. The foolish will lament the lack of recognition – foolish because life does not owe us recognition, and those who receive it are additionally foolish if they derive any satisfaction from it. They have, as Jesus said, their reward: there is nothing more to come. The sensible will concede that their fate is 'just the way things have turned out'. But it can be hugely unsettling for all that. In reality, of course, it is a providential intimation of authentic spirituality. Experience built up, the talents developed, and the expertise learned – whether in running a family home or writing a book – are the beginnings of eternal life. Looked at in this sense the qualities which are durable, that survive our present life and are the building materials of our everlasting habitation, are of cardinal value for their own sake. Their use, their implementation, is part of spiritual formation. The pervasive sense that our experience appears rejected by the world is actually a growth in that detachment from worldly priorities which the Saviour himself commended in the Parable of the Sower. A very great deal of what we have tried to become awaits us in eternity; we should not expect it in this life. Our experience now, all our labour in this life, makes a person who is ready and capable of service in the Kingdom of light.

Now this is the weekend of Whitsun, the celebration of the Holy Spirit, the outpouring of gifts. It is this last which so plainly addresses the condition just described. God calls all sorts of people to his Kingdom – literally *all* sorts. Our different gifts, like our differing degrees of virtue and sin, are inseparable from our common citizenship of Christ's realm. God uses us as we are, that our virtues might be properly directed, and our sins, once acknowledged, forgiven. The Holy Spirit is the infusion of many gifts, and they match and correspond to the many types of talent, expertise and experience which men and women accumulate in life. Instead of being frustrated because the world does not appear to want them, it should be our joy to realize that the very essence of a calling in the Spirit is all about different gifts being employed, not in earthly advancement, but in preparation for an eternal citizenship. As usual, we bring suffering upon ourselves when we trust our own evaluation of our worth. Whitsun is an occasion of great spiritual serenity, for the simplest person with the most residual gifts now finds that the stone which the builders rejected has become the cornerstone, that things of lowly recognition in the world are loved by God in eternity.

Fifteen

The vocation of interpretation

ଧୁଠଔ

Not much is thought of a scholar who selects from his data only those ideas which already coincide with his existing beliefs, or of a scientist who does not bother to consult all available variants to the probabilities already yielded by experiment or calculation. Yet that is precisely what many are prepared to do when deciding about religious truth. They simply do not learn the appropriate methods of enquiry, or realize that it is necessary to re-enter the cultural attitudes of those who formulated the traditions of thought which we have inherited. In biblical terms that means a rediscovery of the use made of images – in the spiritual vocabulary of the prophets, in the teaching of Christ himself. When questioned about the Parable of the Sower, Jesus actually explained both why he taught in images and what the meaning of the particular story was. This method of instruction, which was common in the ancient world, and especially so in the rabbinic style employed by Christ, has the enormous advantage that through the choice of everyday uses and symbols, available to the understanding of everyone, a series of meanings can be communicated simultaneously, in several layers of interpretation. But to understand the teaching it is necessary to hold a number of shared cultural assumptions – and it is these that people today do not bother with. As in so much else in the modern world, if something is not immediately attainable it is not pursued.

Let the point be illustrated by the image of the *rock*, perhaps one of the most common in the Bible. God himself, indeed, is 'the rock of our salvation'. For a people wandering in the desert a rock provides shade and shelter; rocky outcrops store rainwater; caves and fissures are homes, and the resort of solitaries seeking spiritual advance; rocks are dependable building material, and rocky heights can be defended against an enemy. As an image of refuge and dependability, therefore, the rock recurs in the Bible and in the teaching of Jesus. The confession of Jesus as the Christ made by Peter was at Caesarea Philippi: a shrine to Pan and rustic pagan divinities – a huge rock-face carved with symbols of Hellenistic piety. The rock as safety prompted Jesus' story about the man who built his house upon the rock. But the image always carried layers of meaning. For the rock which provides a dwelling also provides a tomb. It is death as well as life; and everywhere there were graves and chambers cut into the rock, like the sepulchre of Christ himself. Peter was the rock, Cephas, on which the Saviour built his Church; he was also, as in the Parable of the Sower, the rock on which the seed fell which became dried up, and failed to germinate. Thus Peter denied Christ at the time of his trial. And there is the great hope for all of us. Our redemption occurs despite the frailties of our natures, if we try to love God and to be faithful to him at the time of trial. The rock of dependence is also the rock which can be barren: it is us. We shall not fully understand the meaning of our calling, however, if we do not bother to learn the spiritual tradition in which it comes to us.

Sixteen

Wheat and tares

ഔര

The presentation of crime as a form of entertainment is not new. The Victorians had a great appetite for 'penny dreadfuls', and the cosy detective novel has an established place in the reading of many people. Children are socialized by 'cops and robbers' games (now under different names) which offer instruction in simple ethical models of behaviour through the demonizing of wrongdoers. All these had an obviously fictionalized context, however, or when centred on real events they had no actual consequences in the administration of justice: they comprised moral exhortation, not attempts to produce direct or popular involvement with the treatment meted out to criminals. But in our own day people are being encouraged to participate in the processes which effect the fate of criminals. Slowly, there is public acceptance of the idea that victims or their relatives should have a voice in sentencing policy; the press sometimes offers opinions on prison 'tariffs'. Popular television programmes in which crime is monitored, and individuals caught on security cameras are held up for identification, are disguised as exercises in public service. In reality they are introductions to street justice – very little removed, in emotional effect, from the gladiatorial exhibitions of antiquity or the sensationalism of public executions. It is not crime as entertainment so much as criminals for entertainment; and it is not Christian.

The number of those thought of as criminals is increasing. This is not due to a moral breakdown or the collapse of family values, as moralists like to think, but is simply because the law is remorselessly extending the definition of crime. In the name of welfare and public decency the minutest details of conduct are being subject to criminalization – mothers who leave young children unattended, minor sexual irregularities, failure to comply with the escalating complexity of financial regulation, drug use, petty acts of violence, and so forth. Many instances of small-scale bad behaviour, which once would have been dealt with inside the family or a social group, are now coming within the competence of the state. More and more people are being convicted. We are living in a new puritanism, with society self-consciously dividing itself between the supposedly virtuous and the evildoers. As a dreadful paradox, many seem to believe this a Christian state of affairs – Christianity understood in an ethicized sense. Yet Christianity recognizes the universality of sin, and the inherent corruption of us all. Apart from a few authentic psychopaths there are no true 'criminal types'; there are just inadequate people, unable to cope, self-seeking, careless of others, in need of forgiveness. When crime is presented as entertainment, criminals are automatically demonized, and we are all then the losers, because a false definition of the nature of humanity itself achieves priority. Christianity recognizes the need for sanctions in the ordering of society precisely because this is a fallen creation. But it recognizes also the moral frailty of us all, and the essential ambiguity of our attempts at virtue.

Seventeen

As we are

ജ

The social and cultural assumptions of the modern world encourage us all to think too highly of ourselves. We see ourselves as endowed with an expansive range of personal rights, and humanity itself as sovereign over the circumstances of life. Compared with the material conditions in which most people on the planet have lived – and many are still living – our condition is actually nothing short of luxurious. But we do not see it that way, and lay claim, indeed, to ever more refined entitlements. Above all, we regard humans themselves as somehow 'sacred', owed a special release from the pain and uncertainties which describe the existence of every other living creature. Yet we also recognize an insufficiency in ourselves individually to arrange all the benefits we expect, and so look to government, to the state, to provide what we want. It is an extraordinary condition to have arrived at: a kind of revolt against reality, a belief in personal exemption from the raw materials of existence. People project 'happiness' as their desired goal. Those who pray often issue a kind of tariff of exemption from pain to God – exemption from illness or accident, from distress and misfortune. We have the authority of the words of Jesus himself, however, for understanding that God knows our needs before we ask; and prayer should anyway have another priority. That most perfect form of prayer given by Jesus began not with a petition but with an acclamation: 'Your name is holy'. People today would do well to recover some sense of that priority. The holiness of God is unlike any quality in humanity itself – about whom there is really very little that is 'sacred'. God transcends the imagination, and the very contemplation of the divine power is in itself liable to make us think again before considering personal happiness as the end of life. So removed from ourselves is the divine nature, in fact, that we are unable to determine some of the most crucial dimensions of the divine purpose – why God made the universe, what human life is for, and what significance should be attached to the rest of created life.

Look again at humanity. We really are not worth saving, and the true miracle of God's love is precisely that he bothers with us. Humanity is far from the modern image of itself: as naturally benign, as possessed of self-evident worth and capable of unflawed reason. We are too impressed by our intellectual and technical discoveries. They should be set against our self-seeking, greed, moral ambiguity, and sheer nastiness. Yet God calls us to share with him in the development of the earth, and on the way to discover ourselves. But the selves we discover should always recognize their difference from the holiness of God. In using the gifts of God we come to think ourselves akin to him, whereas we remain his creatures, limited by the circumstances of our lives and the fearful facts of our natures. If we would see God at work, we should first marvel at a love so great that it is offered freely to a people like us.

Eighteen

The divine mercy

 howcs

Trust is crucial in human relationships, and in the general
operations of society. Even at the petty level of daily exchange,
like the reliability of service or the dependability of transport,
the violation of obligations made on trust can cause distress.
Translated to the more serious matter of personal relationships,
and issues of emotional dependence, the inviolability of trust
involves our most basic human feelings. Within sexual relationships, for example, or in dealings between people who have
committed themselves deeply to some joint enterprise, the
maintenance of trust is recognized as the decisive element for
fruitfulness. Family life is fraught at the best of times, but it is
only through the dependable commission of mutual responsibilities that it works at all. Families appear to dissolve into
recrimination at a very early threshold; think how often the
trigger is an issue in which trust has seemed to have been
violated. Then examples and nagging disagreements going back
for decades are dredged up and used in evidence. Yet trust is
taken for granted, a largely unspoken part of daily life, assumed
as a common decency which all will respect and observe.

The greatest example of trust – indeed it is more than an
example, for it is the foundation of all things – is the faithfulness of God towards us. We take that for granted, too. There
is no person so humble, or so vicious, none, even, who is
unresponsive to the serious purposes of life, to whom God does
not entrust himself. He is beside the murderer in the prison, the
pervert, the faithless, and those whom society find literally
irredeemable. His capacity to give himself to his creatures – so
astounding a gift – was disclosed in the Crucifixion of Christ.

Then God himself, in human reality, entrusted himself forever to human kind, their Saviour and their Friend. He confides the knowledge of his love, and we are charged with the perpetual unfolding of that knowledge, through every generation and place, for all time. How poorly we even recognize that trust, let alone act upon it. Yet we should behave as if – as it does – our life depends upon it. And how sorrowful must the face of Jesus be as he regards our lack of responsiveness. And yet how unreservedly the New Covenant of his Death and Resurrection is kept. So God himself places trust at the centre of life, and we are each called to trust one another in emulation of the great example of the Creator himself. Though we ought to be mortified by our own chilling failure to respond to the sacrificial trust of God, yet we can also achieve the extraordinary serenity of those whose hope is in Christ, and in the company of the celestial society which beckons us. For the supreme disposer of all things – of the vastness of the universe, and of the love which makes a lowly widow share her last coin with a person in still greater need – has not only looked down with pity on the work of his hands: he has entrusted us, as well, with a love that is everlasting.

Nineteen

Getting the context right

ॐ ☙

Until the last couple of centuries or so people had expected life to be hazardous, and were brought up to understand that the world was a dangerous place. Natural afflictions combined with human savagery to make the conditions of existence unreliable and unpredictable. Expectations were in consequence fairly low; people did not make the kind of claims we consider normal to a painless sojourn upon the earth, during which time there are clear entitlements to personal exemption from the evils familiar to the ancients. The advances of science, especially in medicine, energy, and the productive use of nutritional resources, have enabled men and women to assume that life will be progressively more stable and secure. When sickness or natural disaster does occur, indeed, there is now almost an irritated impatience – blame is located in those who could have managed public affairs in a way better calculated to diminish the effects of such incidents. People in traditional society knew better. They had an almost instinctive sense that life was intended to be fragile and transient, and that its spiritual beauty, in fact, derived precisely from the evidences of these qualities, and not – as we think today – from the moral elevation of humanity or its aesthetic accomplishments. The earth's inhabitants in former times were the successors of incredibly ancient knowledge that came echoing down to them through centuries of oral tradition. It told of disasters of the long past, of heavenly bodies falling from the skies, of dreadful and mysterious plagues, of scorching drought. The ancients knew what we, with our recent security, have so rapidly forgotten: that the earth is not stable, that it is not a peaceful home.

We exist, as modern knowledge is now able to inform us, in the middle of a gigantic explosion. The universe is a brief phenomenon, seemingly an explosion in a void. Ageless time, in human observation of the world, is a few seconds of a violent chaos, as everything moves outwards at astonishing speed. Dust and gas momentarily form into shapes and are then consumed – our earth is a brief reality in the thick of the shocking attrition. Bits of debris move randomly about, and occasionally collide. How wise the ancients were to recognize that the world was coming to an end, that it was not eternal. And how right they were to fear the awesome power of Creation. What they also saw, and we see only dimly, was that Creation is the expression of a person, of a creative will. The purpose and meaning of the universe, and of the life which momentarily coats at least one speck of the debris, is not known to us. Nor is the fate that awaits living things. But Christianity is heir to the ancient sense that the Creator of all things can be known, and that, indeed, he calls us to share with him in the creative processes. God is a person, Christians believe, and God is love. In the middle of the unspeakable chaos humanity is able to witness to a serene truth. Forget the yearning for security and personal significance; wonder, instead, at the sheer majesty of God.

Twenty

Forgiveness

൬൬

People tend to write their own agenda – both personal and social – into the message of Jesus. Thus he is made to be one who confers significance upon the various needs of the individual, who promises fulfilment of a list of emotional requisites. In public terms, he becomes the champion of justice and world peace, and brings consolation to the sufferings of humanity. But the essential message of Jesus was actually a call for personal repentance. It was expressed, furthermore, with great urgency: life was not given to each of us to dispose of as we will, but is the occasion to respond to specific commands which God makes; and as life is finite, so the need to recognize that calling is immediate. There is no time to waste. Men and women are not sufficient in themselves to procure their own amendment, and what is wrong with them is at the very centre of their being – it is not some accident of conditioning, or incidental wrong choice produced by defective social environment, or the injustices of human organization. In the very heart of people there is a flaw which somehow effects our every action; it defines us as creatures who are less than the Creator, and whose capacity for self-correction is limited. Humanity, by definition in fact, is faulty. That is very definitely not what the modern world wants to hear. For we have come to estimate mankind as the centre of all things, and the needs of people and their claims as sovereign. The greatest good modern people can imagine is human welfare, and our moral culture has been reduced to a welfare programme. Jesus, however, as he moved among the people and taught them of the love of God, began by setting out an essential pre-condition for salvation: they must repent. They must, that is to say, confess that they are not, in their own strength, capable of lifting themselves out of the dreadful moral ambiguity and actual wrongdoing that describes normal human conduct. Yet modern people do not recognize such a description of themselves – they have a notably exulted view of their capacity for contriving change, both personal and social. The change produced in people who submit to the rule of Christ, furthermore, relates to their spiritual condition and is not a transformation of their humanity – which remains flawed. That is particularly hard for modern people to understand. For, as in everything else, they look for instant results, consumer spirituality, a religion which appears to work by making people morally better.

What those who repent become, however, is not transformed in human terms – but forgiven. It is quite unreal and a defiance of the nature of reality as set up by the Creator to expect a kind of magic reconstitution of the personality. Obedience to God signals a spiritual condition that has changed – it makes our merely human failings, which continue, even more seriously hazardous to our spiritual integrity, but it does not eradicate them. Having become people who are forgiven, in addition, we have the obligation to forgive others, as the Lord's Prayer commands. Spirituality involves the evolution of a universal network of forgiveness, our invisible communion of the blessed which is the very beginning of knowing how to love God.

Twenty One

Keeping the truth

ೞಚ

One of the most significant changes that has occurred in religion in Western countries over the last couple of centuries has been the removal of social impulsions encouraging observance. In traditional society religion was a mark of communal identity and social loyalty; it did not have to 'appeal' to people individually since it represented the collective subscription of society generally to higher purposes for human life. The religion conveyed in this way did not have to satisfy emotional needs or cater to personal claims to significance or meaning. It was true in itself, and the organization of society was witness to its authority: the commands of God were the ethical basis of human association. One consequence was that conversion from one religion to another involved radical statements about the nature of the state – hence the truly heroic stances of those, in the early Church for example, who accepted a new religious allegiance. This whole vision of things has now disappeared within Christianity, though it is fast reviving in Islam. Modern people are accustomed to privatized religion, and see it as an unquestionable right to pick and choose among available systems, or not to bother at all. The long-term effects of the Romantic movement in taste, furthermore, have simultaneously added the notion that religious belief is emotionally enriching, and that individuals can judge religious faith by the degree to which it assists uplift and a sense of beauty or serenity. Religion as therapy was born out of the idea that belief brought personal benefits which had little to do with the traditional obligations of obeying God because his commandments are true. To modern people religious belief has to be comforting, palliative, bearing the promise of individual healing, a consolation against the ills of existence.

The Churches, alas, show every sign of having adopted this understanding of religion themselves. They speak in marketing terms, of the 'appeal' of faith, of the 'need' which people have, of the benefit of 'fulfilled' lives. The current confusion of aesthetics and spirituality assists this: virtually anything which promotes a 'higher' dimension to life, virtually any human accomplishment in the arts, is regarded as somehow an indication of human religiosity. Serious music and serious art is acclaimed as witnessing, even if anonymously, to a divine inspiration. Children in schools are encouraged to suppose that moral consciousness and 'caring' attitudes are the very quintessence of religious faith. Marketing religion for a market society may well prove disastrous for authentic religion, however. The commands of God are not naturally appealing, and the way of the Cross is hard and often extremely unpleasant. At the centre of Christianity is a structure of doctrine, not a beautiful sentiment. It is about the evil of humanity and the need for men and women to repent; about the mercy of God, who forgives those who call upon him by making real sacrifices of their worldly preferences. The truths of religion are not just picked up at random selection – they have to be learned and applied. And that is not a message which the modern world will want to hear.

Twenty Two

Fallen creatures

౮౦౧౩

As 'caring' more and more supersedes holiness as the model proposed by modern society as the ideal for humanity, it is curious to have to note the disagreeable truth that individuals actually tend to show a diminished evidence of either in their own conduct. They turn to the state and its agencies to take on the messy task of looking after others, and are outraged when their own quality of life is interfered with by social duties which in former times were regarded as inseparable from normal living. Thus unwanted babies are routinely aborted, and elderly relatives are shuffled 'into care' (to use the chilling euphemism of the times) if there is any prospect that lifestyles will be interrupted should they be left around. Behind this dreadful tendency lies the wrong priorities of modern men and women; their conception of human existence as the pursuit of personal happiness and the open-ended entitlement to 'fulfilment'. There are, of course, still numerous examples of sacrificial lives – of those who take parenthood to be a distinct vocation, and of those whose lives are dedicated to the personal care of dependent relatives. In general, however, the movement of things towards acceptance of the notion that the state has the obligation to relieve individuals of unwanted obligations, and that lives should be left unimpeded by irritations and ex-responsibilities, gains ground daily.

The paramount cause here is the supremacy of *welfare:* the highest ideal of moral seriousness today, the sanctification of modern political consciousness, the goal of a 'caring' moral environment. Having marginalized the demands of God, or having ceased to believe in him, people today find in 'caring' and the public sacralizing of 'welfare' an apparently adequate substitute. Here they can release all the censoriousness which once gave rise to Puritanism; in welfare issues there can now be found most of the leading values of the age. Transcendence has long been secularized: people now possess little acquaintance with the requirements of an unseen world of divine priorities; instead they simulate the emotional effects in the supposedly 'higher' dimensions of art and music. Religious faith itself is sometimes converted by its own devotees into the new currency, and loses its objective basis of obedience to the divine will and becomes merely an emotional affair of sugared 'caring'. The common defining element in all this is the sovereignty of human life – the sense that the material fate of people is much more important than ultimate truths about the nature of existence. It is shown in the impatience people have with religious conflicts when they encounter them as news items, whether it is among Catholics and Protestants in Northern Ireland, Orthodox and Moslems in the Balkans, or fundamentalist Hindus in India. How can people, they seem to say, regard religion as more important than human welfare? Add intellectual relativism and the mixture can be recognized for what it is: authentic materialism. The saints and scholars of the Christian tradition must weep as they behold it all from eternity.

Twenty Three

The hope of sinners

Sin is a fact of human life; it is, indeed, one of the facts with which everyone has a daily acquaintance. It is not just that we fall into the commission of evil acts, but that our very being expresses the inherent presence of sinfulness. Capable of advances of knowledge which mark us off from the rest of the Creation and make us like the angels, we are simultaneously degraded by flaws which make all our actions ambiguous and many of them downright wrong. This is the very nature of humanity, and it is unchanging. No advances of self-knowledge or manipulation of the environment can alter it; nothing we do can control it. At the end of time itself men and women will be as they are now: creatures permanently in need of amendment. The casual optimism about human capabilities which describes modern assumptions about our nature – and which is strangely held by a people who are conscious as never before, because of the accessibility of information, of the dreadful things that men and women can do – impedes realistic acceptance of personal sinfulness. It seems such a dated concept. We prefer to think of wrong choices made by people, or, even better, of circumstances which account for wrongdoing. There are, however, some exceptions. Whatever modern people really are induced to regard as evil – child abuse for example, or racial violence – they set in a special category. The perpetrators of these evils become 'beasts' or 'animals', language which itself suggests that they are outside humanity. Humanity, that is to say, is by definition incapable of such things.

But sin is universal; its level is the same in everyone. The apparent differences in people indicate variations of location.

Some express their sinfulness in child abuse, some in malice, and some in persistent insensitivity to the feelings of others. Virtuous lives are not characterized by the absence of sin; they are achieved by those who, conscious of the ineradicable truth about their corrupted natures, nevertheless seek occasions for offering up their faults in some kind of service or interior expiation. We should not be impressed by the external signs of virtue in others: lives which convention scorns may yet be characterized by internal nobility – itself striving against inherent evil to seek goodness. There is a small category of people (sometimes regarded, superstitiously, as 'possessed' by evil) who really do seem to lack the inherent conflict of sin and virtue which is the normal human condition. It is not easy to know what to make of them, how to judge their condition. Most people have at some point in their lives encountered one or two who are truly malicious, and who are in this small category. Offer it, and offer them, up to a higher understanding; do not be drawn in by trying to engage them. Humanity is united by its shared sinfulness, and it is united also, though it often does not realize it, by God's mercy. Jesus came into the world to forgive sin. After acceptance of his forgiveness our inherent sinfulness remains – but so does the mercy of God.

Twenty Four

———

The year ahead

୫୦୦୫

The arrival of a new year is not likely to be greeted with unmixed anticipation of fresh opportunities and optimistic predictions. People stocktake their lives and assess their possible fate in the months that stretch before them. The present is a time of global uncertainty: the new configurations of national claims and resurgent social problems are very different from those which characterized the Cold War era; the incoherence is all the more alarming because of the absence of any clear purpose in Western societies. Many problems are still, for all that, old problems – or were here in other guises before; and it is we, in each successive generation, who are new to them. But the disappearance of any higher destiny for human society to look to *is* new, and is an important departure. It is disguised by rhetoric about human rights and democratic values and welfare, and by the extraordinary capacity of an educated people to seem satisfied with short-term assessments of the future of culture. Almost all the philosophical and religious convictions which once determined the purposes behind social organization have been individualized and privatized – and in consequence have been marginalized. Few now suppose that the purpose of society is the Creation or protection of a pattern of living which evokes superior divine intentions for humanity; it is rare, these days, to find much serious thought about the theoretical bases of the political order and the ideas which institutions are intended to encourage and to promote. Instead, the observer beholds vaunted substitutes for thought: the priority in political idealism of welfare, security, democracy. The supremacy of economic issues, not only in political discourse but also in popular expectations, is clear evidence of the condition of Western peoples. Theirs is the lower ground, the materialist assumption that human life is all about immediate matters of self-interest.

At the personal level, too, so many people reflect the larger condition. Lives are passed in unreflective inconsequence, with little to encourage the pursuit of higher goals. The avoidance of suffering and the promotion of individual well-being appear to be the controlling passions of the generality – set in the context of a scramble for security, and orchestrated greed. People are full of anxiety. Those who no longer envisage their lives as occasions of sacrifice, or as chances for showing enterprise in serving higher ideals, are inevitably eaten up with fear that the things which they *do* value – personal self-interest and freedom from pain – are threatened. The level of protection they seek against the ordinary hazards of existence is simply not available. No matter what men and women may do, life on earth will always be full of uncertainties, and their unreasonable claims for personal exemption will in the end always be mocked by fate. 'Do not lay up for yourselves treasure upon earth, where moth and rust corrupt': the words of Jesus are addressed to our condition with terrifying precision. Fear is the dominant feature of the lives of those who ignore him – fear for security, for survival, and for their fate in a seemingly darkening future.

Twenty Five

Not us, but God

ℰℭ

The modern attempt to promote religious belief by appeal to the personal and emotional *needs* of potential adherents is more likely, taking a long view, to diminish the amount of authentic Christianity than to increase it. People are told that religion will 'fill a gap' in their lives, that it will provide emotional enrichment, satisfy the craving for personal significance, elicit sensations of human warmth. Those addressed in this manner are often only too ready to agree that religion is indeed by its nature intended to supply these benefits. For they are now accustomed to considering religious belief as a matter of immediate personal choice – without the associations of communal identity and obligation it once involved – and as a kind of entitlement, rather like going on welfare. It is the market applied to evangelism, and derives ultimately from the impact of the Evangelical Revival at the end of the eighteenth century, which emphasized personal emotion in the perception of religious truth, and from the leisure revolution of the twentieth century, when religion became, like everything else, something available to entertain the individual in spare time.

Modern people expect religion to do something for them. There were precursors of this in traditional peasant religion, when the divinities and the saints were thought to assist daily labour – like St Isidore the Labourer, helped by an angel as he struggled with his plough. Others sought prosperity and material blessings from prayer. It might have seemed that such primitivism had been expunged from Christianity, but it is alive and well within the expectations of many today. Now, however, what is demanded of religion is emotional satisfaction.

Traditional Christianity was a structure of doctrine, a matter of subscription to precise forms which the individual did not expect to adjust to suit his own emotional preferences. It expressed obligations owed to God and involved not emotional fulfilment, but privation. People today like to be highly selective about which parts of religious doctrine they will choose to adopt; they become, in fact, angry if ecclesiastical authorities point out – when they still have the temerity or inclination to do so – that Christianity has some indispensable and fixed doctrinal references which are not negotiable against a personalized scheme determined by individual disposition. Church leaders who attempt to present religion to the public as a product to be sold on its appeal, as an advertising agent might do, are simply being unfaithful to the very doctrines they are supposed to hold in trust. Religion does not 'appeal', and it is founded not in emotional need but in objective truths, many of which are deeply antipathetic to what humans regard as their entitlements. At the centre of Christianity is the assurance of its Founder that there is something wrong in the hearts of men and women, and that what we need is not some pandering to our emotional greed but a structure of spiritual discipline. Religion is about giving things up. It is about denying ourselves things, including emotional entertainment, so that we may follow Christ into the austerities of the wilderness – and therefore into the clarity of the light by which we can see light.

Twenty Six

The true cost of virtue

ᛒᏂᏟᏜ

At the centre of the Christian life is service. God is served by us not only directly, through the offering of perpetual praise, but indirectly by serving one another. The one who is greatest in the Kingdom of Heaven is also the one who is most lowly in the world – who is, as Christ made himself, the servant of others. It is easily said and much less easily fulfilled, partly because the concept of service for its own sake is largely absent from modern consciousness. In our society the notion of *service* has been replaced by that of *caring*. They are not the same thing. 'Caring' is, anyway, rather a rhetorical device, employed as a synonym for moral probity in a highly selective fashion. Although children are exhorted in school, for example, to become 'caring' people, and to exhibit 'caring' natures, the actual content of what caring implies is rather vaguely rendered – and would seem to involve respecting the beliefs of others provided those beliefs may be considered politically correct. It would also seem to involve the performance of such good works as the individual could reasonably expect to receive in return. Caring is thus an exercise in calculated hedonism, derived from an unstated ideological position. If an enquirer should ask (though few in practice do) of what theoretical or ideological system these caring acts are an application, he would not receive a coherent answer. For there is not one. To identify a basis in religious morality, for example, would offend against that dogma of political correctness which contends that all religious positions are of equal validity; to argue for a basis in traditional cultural inheritance would likewise encounter the claim that all cultures are to be venerated. The modern concept of caring in fact derives from the secular elevation of humanity; it is an undefined Humanism, and is an almost perfect expression of the materialists' conviction that people are to be respected for their humanity rather than because of any rules derived from their transcendence. The equivalent disposition in the ancient world was 'common decency', and was regarded then as the lowest level of human responsibility, without which a man was a barbarian. Our predecessors would have been astounded that such a minimal practice of human decency should, after a couple of thousand years, be taught to children as the highest good.

Christian service, in contrast, is the application of a theology. People are to be served because they are God's children, and not out of supposedly enlightened self-interest. Christian service is the enactment of belief in higher purposes for human life, and it is due to God before it is due to ourselves. At its heart is self-denial, in order that the practitioner should recognize a personal culture which belongs to God – the very ownership of the personality by God. Service is for its own sake, but it is not an end in itself. It is sacrificial, for it denies the priority of personal need in order that the Christ conveyed in others may be served.

Twenty Seven

Power from on high

୫୨୦ଓଃ

A great deal is written and said about the complexities of life in modern society, and much of it is true. But men and women are extremely adaptable, and in general they can manage to find themselves at home in the successive shifts of culture and of circumstance. It is as well to remember this, because those charged with the transmission of beliefs and values to future generations, like leaders in religion, have the obligation to sift the really essential truths, which are everlasting, from the cultural accretions which adhere in each passing moment. Their duty is to think in terms of centuries, not mere years; and when it comes to the determination of what Christianity is all about, a long rather than a short perspective is really essential. It is notably lacking among modern Church leaders, at least within the Protestant Churches, whose agenda for deciding Christian priorities is frequently set by the immediate passions of humanity. The adaptability possessed by men and women relates to domesticating themselves in the world, however, and in their natures they are unchanging. Now at the centre of the Christian view of things is a statement about the condition of humanity which is as unflattering about its spiritual and moral capabilities as it is at variance with the self-esteem of humanity today. Dazzled by the ability to devise technology, men and women ignore the fact that they are not capable of reconstructing themselves – indeed, even if they could, they would not know how to begin to agree about a programme of regeneration. The world is full of competing religions and moral systems. It is also true that for most ordinary people there are not endless problems of higher choice and decision, but a simple difficulty about coping with the immediate problems of life on a daily basis.

The world wants to be flattered on its own terms. It was always so. People want to be assured that humanity matters in some absolute and sovereign sense, and that they are in the end capable of arranging their own destinies. In the secularized understanding of the Western intelligentsia, and those whom they influence, the reality of God has been laid aside and in his place is the sovereignty of humanity. It is a list of 'Human Rights' which now occupies the centre-stage of the human drama, not the service of a Creator; people think in terms of a decade or so, at best, rather than in terms of centuries. Modern society is not even attempting to pass on eternal values to its successors, but is content, instead, with proclaiming the material welfare of men and women themselves as the highest good. Men and women, as it happens, have no inherent dignity in virtue of their human qualities – which are, indeed, permanently flawed – but because God loves the work of his hands. The astonishing thing about human society is not any technical accomplishments it may have contrived, or any great art and music, or whatever, but that God bothers with it. Humanity does not have any 'rights' in such a context. It has only the duty of obedience and gratitude: to a God whose mercy is far greater than anything that we can even imagine.

Twenty Eight

Dust to dust

ଚ୨୯ଓ

Religious belief has always been associated with the supernatural, and it cannot be doubted that some today turn to
Christianity in anticipation of an experience of supernatural
forces. There is a worryingly pervasive fascination with the idea
of paranormal phenomena in modern society, as evidence in
the popularity of television series on these themes. People who
would be ashamed to believe in magic in normal circumstances
appear to revel in it when it is presented as science fiction. The
clergy will confirm that many who consult them are primarily
interested in the supernatural dimension of what they think
of as Christianity. The miraculous events described in the Bible,
and the miracles attributed to Christ himself, seem to testify
to the authenticity of supernatural powers within religion;
ecclesiastical miracles have been recorded evenly across the
history of the Churches. Many believe they can communicate
with the dead, and even more look to prayer as a means of
actually rearranging reality in order to achieve desired ends.
But God has called men and women to work with him in the
progressive development of the Creation, and has endowed
them with the faculties of reason and reflection to enable them
to do so. Prominent in their consequent discoveries are
accounts of earthly phenomena which increasingly exclude the
likelihood of supernatural forces determining actual events.

The universe which God created is 'natural', and so, therefore,
is our world and all its phenomena – including us. Everything
operates according to laws and probabilities which may ultimately be known, or at least conjectured, since the Creation is
'real' and not an illusion. There is no need for 'supernatural'

explanation: God has revealed his purposes – whose grand design we cannot know – in the Creation, and it is our only source of knowledge. There are no mysterious intimations or visions which do not derive from our own material constitution. The philosophical materialists are right to the extent that they explain how matter has determined our perception of ourselves and of the world; they are wrong in supposing that this 'natural' order is without design or purpose. Christians believe that the universe expresses a will, and accept with humility the otherwise galling fact that humans cannot know *all* that is willed by the Creator. Science is showing that the universe is a less predictable place than had previously been supposed, and that the laws of matter (if it is still possible to use such a phrase) involve more apparently arbitrary aspects than mechanistic thought had allowed. But, taken all-in-all, reality must now be seen as a 'natural' series of phenomena. Christians believe that the Creator, in wishing to make himself known to his creatures, became himself, at an historical moment, a part of the Creation. Christ stood outside of the created order and yet was of its substance: this is the central truth and the cardinal paradox of the Christian religion. We are invited, as natural beings in a world that operates naturally, to follow his teaching and to love the things which he loved. We are also required, as persons of reason and reflection, to emancipate the divine from the merely human in the circumstances of his life on earth, and to recognize in Jesus a person who, alone, transcended material reality in a great revelation of the Divine love.

Twenty Nine

Raised to glory

ઇ૭൏ଓ

The Feast of the Ascension, celebrated last week, should not be marginalized, or explained in symbolic language, as modern Church leaders are inclined to do. It marks a decisive moment in the purpose of the Incarnation itself, and is inseparable from the Resurrection. If Christ really did rise from the grave his departure from the world must have been equally miraculous – equally at variance with previous experience. Legends have always persisted that he remained alive, and some have sought to identify his tomb: an indication of credulity rather than authenticity. For Christians the proof of the Resurrection and the Ascension, and the confirmation of the promises made to his followers by the risen Christ, is the existence of the Church itself – his body in the world. The life of Jesus, and the fact of his Resurrection, plainly involved 'miraculous' events, and it is not possible to accept the claims of Christianity without acknowledging them. But when God himself, the Creator of all things, was in the world and sharing in its very substance, the laws which ordinarily describe the acts of humans are not applicable. The works of healing performed by Christ were within the expectations of those who followed him; they were intended, like the Incarnation itself, to make the heavenly knowable in human terms – in terms of what humans expected of religious phenomena. They were done with a certain reserve, a kind of concession to human understanding; Jesus himself wearied of the popular desire for 'a sign' or for 'wonders', but recognized that they were part of the spiritual culture of the ancient world.

The central events of the life of Christ – the Virgin Birth, the descent of the dove at his Baptism, the Resurrection and the Ascension – were of a different nature, however. These were not folk miracles, given in order to convey or signify religious authority in the manner expected by those who heard Jesus, and therefore comparable to those supposedly performed by many spiritual leaders as evidence of their charism. The central miracle of the Incarnation itself and its consequences were unique. When God was in the world as a person the distinction between the 'supernatural' and the 'natural' disappeared, for the Creator of all things was, as it were, creating as he went along: yet he was fully a man – a man using the expectations of his day to convey his message and authority. This was a long way from the notion, so widespread today, as in the past, that all religious experience involves an acquaintance with the 'supernatural', and that reality today can be changed by religious faith. The most perfect form of prayer given by Jesus to his followers was devoid of petitions for miraculous cures or personal exemptions from physical hazards – the substance of so many prayers offered by modern people. We live in a real creation, not a magic sideshow; in the world God is known about through the natural order. He is also and supremely known in Christ, the great focus of revealed truth. God's presence in Christ was, in our terms, 'miraculous'. Our lives, in contrast, are 'natural', and the world we inhabit operates wholly through the material order established by God.

Thirty

Making a good end

ഇരു

The manner in which people regard death relates a great deal about how they evaluate life. To many today the elevation of humanity and its needs above the ancient notion that life exists for higher purposes than our welfare, has reached a point where death itself seems a kind of blasphemy. We exalt ourselves so thoroughly that we cannot conceive of an order of things in which our desires are not sovereign. Translated beyond the grave this means that those who believe in survival after death – probably a large majority – reject the idea that, in a future state, they will experience anything but uninterrupted bliss. When life is considered as the endless pursuit of happiness, and the indulgences of pleasure are imagined to be the greatest good, it is scarcely surprising that a serene eternal life should be claimed as a normal extension of worldly existence. Modern people are universalists. In their picture of the afterlife there is happiness all round, no judgement, and a limitless continuation of familiar human relationships. Few see a connection between *belief* and survival; seemingly any religious opinions are acceptable to God. More, doubtlessly, see a connection between good moral *behaviour* and survival, but it is always other people's behaviour, rather than their own, which merits eternal condemnation. Death is regarded as a potentially minor interruption to the pursuit of happiness, no longer linked to judgement. The moral culture which no longer allows discrimination between ethnic groups, different cultures, personal lifestyles, sexual habits, or even religious belief, does not, equally, discriminate between those who have attempted a disciplined spirituality and those who have not.

After death, we seem to be saying, it is eternal happiness all round.

This actually raises fearful problems for the priest attending a death. His traditional duty was to remind the dying person of the need for repentance, to assist an act of contrition, and to warn about the certainty of God's judgement. Such a duty, performed today, would be considered enormously insensitive by the relatives. Death has to be sanitized; everyone has to be assured that they will receive everlasting blessedness. Do modern people really think that? Do they really think so highly of themselves that they believe they deserve to exist forever? Apparently so; it is no longer acceptable for a priest to remind the dying that they stand in urgent need of God's mercy, but only, instead, to utter bland words of reassurance. The terrors of death remain, however, and the sugared attempts to disguise the horrific fact of universal judgement sound unconvincing even as they are being made. For life has a purpose. That purpose is the service of God. We all do it badly, but to think that we are entitled to exemption from judgement, however we have used our time in the world, is simple folly.

Thirty One

How to know God

෨෦ශ

In the ancient Jewish understanding of things God operated through a particular culture and national experience to reveal his nature. Truth cannot be known if it is rendered in terms which are too generalized: it needs particular expressions and embodiments. In Christianity, which is rooted in the Jewish spiritual tradition, God revealed himself by becoming a man – the supreme example of universal truth assuming a particular form in order to be known. Modern people, in contrast, are sceptical of localized renditions of truth and prefer the general. They claim, for example, a love of humanity. But no one can love humanity, because it is too various and too ambiguous; it is only possible to love individual humans. Preference for the general over the particular suits a people like us, who are wary of ideology and think it is mature to be pragmatic. Mass education, the information explosion, the virtues supposedly annexed to democratic practice, have encouraged modern people to imagine they are 'thinking for themselves' when they decide about what they are to believe. In reality, as it happens, these very conditions have only provided an extremely effective means of mass manipulation of opinion, and the numbers of those who genuinely 'think for themselves' are doubtless as small as they have always been in proportion to the population as a whole. The pervasive sense that mature people will be impatient of precise definitions of truth is, however, only applied in relation to religion and the philosophic bases of public policy. People today are very precise, and insist on very minute definitions, about the agenda of 'political correctness', or what constitutes social behaviour, or Human Rights.

The Church has a problem with all this, even though it usually chooses not to address it directly. Christian truth is the truth revealed in Christ – who did not ruminate in imprecise terms about spiritual beauty or the loveliness of mankind, but delivered a stark rebuke to a generation which was neglecting the laws of God. Christ was the universal in the particular form of a man. It is difficult to imagine a more precise way of conveying exact truths, and Christianity, accordingly, is a religion which requires exclusive allegiance from its adherents. Modern people like to suppose that there is 'truth in all religions', and that men and women should, in effect, adopt the religion suited either to their personal needs or to their encompassing culture. They are largely ignorant of the doctrines of Christianity, and take them to be all about mere human decency; this hugely assists the process of relativizing the religion. Christianity is also undermined by the simultaneous assault upon its historical authority made by emphasizing what is perceived as a record of persecuting others and encouraging warfare – choosing to ignore the comparable, perhaps greater, records of all other religions, and of all peoples at all times. Among the things Christianity is precise about is the sinful state of men and women, including those who seek to serve Christ despite the inherent corruptions of their nature. All religions are *not* of equal value, neither are they simply localized variations of a universal truth. In Christianity the people of the world are offered individual salvation, and that is a very particular and a very precise gift.

Thirty Two

———

Not having everything

ಸಾೀ

Self-denial is not very greatly recognized or practised as a virtue in our society. Indeed, it is scarcely recognized at all – except, perhaps, to the extent that certain habits or the consumption of certain foods, for example, may impair health. The reason for self-denial, in such cases, in plainly self-interest and relates to material well-being. Occasionally self-denial is conceded as a necessary condition for securing the liberties of others, and then, again, it is self-interest which promotes acceptance. The young are exhorted to save instead of spending on credit to obtain desired goods, and here, once again, the intention is not really moral or spiritual formation: it is to spare them the pain of subsequent debt – the motive is practical. The lives of so many today are passed in a gentle self-indulgence which would have shocked our predecessors, and which stands, incidentally, in dreadful contrast to the unavoidable privations of existence in large parts of the developing world. Our culture now contains nothing which suggests that self-denial may be virtuous for its own sake, and the religious teaching which once considered it an important aspect of the spiritual life has largely been abandoned – even amongst those who still adhere to Christianity. We regard ourselves as entitled to the good life; whatever may be deemed an enhancement of that – provided it has no material disadvantages – is judged a kind of birthright. Rights, in fact, have a lot to do with it: the moral culture of rights, with the catalogue of Human Rights at its centre, is hardly likely to honour personal privation, even when voluntarily entered into. Life itself, however it is arranged by social need or political contrivance, is about *not* having what we want. Most would probably say that their priority is happiness: freedom from illness, stable and secure relationships, personal comfort, emotional satisfaction, and so forth – the very areas where self-indulgence may so easily be practised with scarcely any consciousness that moral harm is being done to the individual. For these are also the areas which feed upon themselves, where expectations are forever extending, and where satisfaction proves illusory. To seek self-discipline in the small aspects of personal living is to cultivate moral and spiritual awareness of the need for the same quality in larger matters; self-denial becomes the essential precursor of enlightenment. It is almost impossible to declare this in a society which denies itself nothing. But Christianity has always recognized it. Jesus told his followers to take up their Cross; truth was achieved not by the easy declamation of general principles but by arranging individual lives so that the manner in which a person lives assists spiritual understanding. The world is a place where lessons are to be learned; it is not an interlude of hedonism before everlasting bliss. What we become through the accumulation of spirituality here is what endures for eternity

Thirty Three

More than human need

∞൬

This summer a sizeable group of Christian activists toured several Middle Eastern countries begging the Islamic inhabitants to forgive them for the Crusades. And it is evidently not only modern Christian believers who find the notion of warfare on behalf of religious truth offensive; so do very many among the Western intelligentsia, and it is now held, indeed, that religion itself has been discredited by its association with violence – and not only in the distant past, like the Crusades, but in Northern Ireland or the Balkans. People who really *do* believe in their values, however, defend them at high cost. The NATO war in Kosovo is a case in point. This was trumpeted by its advocates as 'the first moral war in history', fought not out of any national self-interest but in the name of Humanity. It was ethical foreign policy in practice. In reality, of course, it was just another example of a war waged for religion – for the tenets of the secular religion of Humanity. The war in Kosovo fits perfectly into the long list of religious wars as soon as it is recognized that the modern veneration of human life has in effect succeeded Christianity as the moral basis of Western society.

It is actually very important to realize this. For Christians themselves are among the first to absorb the religion of Humanity without any clear consciousness that what they are about is the secularization of their own religious beliefs. God is being replaced by man and his needs as the first priority. Life itself is becoming more important than what individuals exist to believe. Religion is being relegated to the realm of mere emotional satisfaction and therapeutic support, or is understood as a set of ethical principles. It is human need which now occupies the centre of public consciousness of a 'higher' purpose. Whereas religion is judged divisive and full of seemingly archaic precision ('dogma'), concern for human life, which everyone can agree about, unites men and women from different societies and projects achievable goals in the general ideals of justice and peace. How easily this is all made to correspond to basic Christianity! Once all the precise commands of God about the requirement of individual repentance, and all the obligation of worship, have been syphoned off, the residue of ethicism can so readily be equated with the Christian love of neighbour. But there is a problem: Jesus did *not* say that human life was sacred, the way we do; he did *not* declare human need as the essential spring of moral action; and he was *not* indiscriminate about the Divine – very much not. If we would be followers of Christ we must give up placing ourselves and our own estimate of our entitlements at the heart of human life, and recognize, instead, that what Jesus spoke about was our moral frailty and our personal corruption. The whole point about the divine redemption of humanity was that humanity did not deserve it. The miracle of God's love is that he cares for us *despite* ourselves. The beginning of religious wisdom is the consciousness of human sin. Instead, we set too high an estimate on our own lives. Jesus was not a Human Rights activist but a Saviour; he did not come to inform us that our lives were sacred, but that we need forgiveness.

Thirty Four

Remembrance

ଈୠଔଓ

What exactly is being remembered on Remembrance Sunday? It is certainly lost lives, but is it also in some sense a commemoration of the causes for which people died? This would often seem to be implied when the lives sacrificed in the Second World War are linked with the triumph of democracy or the defeat of Nazism. But the custom today is to use Remembrance Sunday as the occasion to remember *all* the war dead, on all the various sides of what was a series of multiple conflicts – of Japanese as well as of Americans in the Pacific, of Germans as well French or Russian or British in Europe. And that is surely the right thing to do. Most of those who died in the wars of this century have been conscripts. Theirs was involuntary sacrifice for they had no control over their destiny and were not consulted, even in democratic countries, about the justice of the causes for which they eventually died. In many ways this makes their heroism even more admirable, and the tragedy of their slaughter all the more to be marked by national recognition. For the moral value of an act is not diminished because the morality is compulsory: law does not cease to be moral because we are obliged to obey it. Genuinely free agency is a very rare commodity indeed in human life, since so much of what we do is determined by conditions over which we have no choice, and even apparently self-conscious choice is in reality filtered by the false consciousness inseparable from all personal formation. Those who die in warfare are serving on our behalf, as agents of the state, in furtherance of ideals or policies which some may, and some may not, believe in. Their sacrifice is the nobler for being made without ideological preconditions.

Remembrance is most valuable, therefore, when it centres on the individual, on the actual soldier or sailor or airman, who lived and breathed and belonged to a family and loved a home and had hopes of better things. It is an occasion to recall particular people over the long passage of the years, so that they will briefly be alive again in our memory – or, as in the case of younger generations, in the imaginings of those who have been told about them. Every child who has had no possibility of personal acquaintance with one of the war dead might be encouraged to 'adopt' a name from a local war memorial, and commend its owner to the mercy of God and the everlasting gratitude of those who survive. For Remembrance is also a time to remind ourselves that the wrath of men and women is not God's way, and that human society, however organized and whatever good or evil may attach to its actions, stands under God's judgement and needs his forgiveness. That is why Remembrance is devalued if it becomes a mere adjunct of 'civic religion', as it so easily does in Britain. Then it loses its vital function of recalling the memory of the real people who are its purpose. The dead can only live again, in earthly terms, if we allow them to be present in our thoughts.

Thirty Five

Family values

෨෦ඎ

Christian sanction is now conventionally given to the maintenance of the family as an essential condition for a properly
constituted society. This is reasonable enough, especially since
there really is no alternative: people either live together in
voluntary units with their own primary loyalties – which is
what family life is – or they are organized by external bodies,
probably institutions of the state in a collectivist polity like ours.
The latter has been tried on many occasions in history and is
plainly inapplicable in our circumstances. The current volatility
of family units, however, is not a pointer to the break-up of
family life as such, as so many seem to think, but only to the fact
that some individuals reassemble family groups less formally
than has been considered either desirable or moral in the
past of the culture. One-parent families, serial relationships,
and same-sex liaisons are not actually destructive of the idea
of the family: they reconstitute it on a different basis and without certain legal constraints and guarantees. Only a very few
really experiment with communal living, and those who do
quickly become categorized as weird, 'hippy' survivors of sixties
liberation, self-sufficiency freaks, enemies of decency. So when
the Churches identify conventional family life as a Christian
model they are still talking about a norm. But what do they
mean?

The 'family' used in the present eulogy of 'family values' –
which is projected as the guardian of moral order and the
essential means of raising children in stable conditions – is
a very recent concept. It is also a class concept. The family,
in this sense, describes the aspirations and social practices of

---

the Western bourgeoisie in the period between about 1880 and about 1960. This was when children were endowed with a romantic innocence quite at variance with observable reality; when 'respectability' withdrew the young from the socializing of the streets which their working-class contemporaries still received; when marriage ceased to be a social arrangement, and when the intended partners raised expectations of romantic love and shared interests; when middle-class families retreated behind net curtains and family life privatized itself. What we call 'the family' today is actually an enormously complicated phenomenon, but its broad characteristic is the assumption that family members will experience the increasingly diverse choices offered by modern culture as a unit. This, as it happens, is clearly difficult to achieve. People are now too individualized to be content with life in the hothouse of the idealized family unit: mass education, heightened expectations to varied experience, the application of consumer instincts to the acquisition of values and lifestyles themselves, sexual freedom, and early maturation of children, cultural diversity, and numerous other considerations are progressively dismantling the bourgeois ideal of the family at a rate which is alarming the moralists. But they need not take fright. Humans are extraordinarily adaptable, and they are already rearranging themselves in perfectly viable alternative modes. Christians in Africa, with the approval of the Lambeth Conference, have acclaimed polygamy as an acceptable lifestyle. Adjustment to received notions of the family in Britain, after that, seems quite mild.

Thirty Six

The mote and the beam

ಬಂಆ

It is common for friends or relatives of someone accused of a fearful crime to say that they know them well and that they are utterly incapable of the evils attributed to them. There is an understandable and wistful humanity in this; but it is unrealistic. All of us are capable of just about anything, given the appropriate circumstances. It is widely acknowledged that in a general breakdown of order – in some apocalyptic vision of a post-nuclear war, for example – people would fend for themselves with little regard for traditional moral constraint. Yet the conditions for such a suspension of moral regularity occur in individual lives, in less dramatic form, all the time. It may well be a matter of chance and opportunity, as much as of moral fortitude and personal nobility of character, whether or not the actions which result offend law and convention. Here is another example of the universality of sin. Humanity is by definition corrupted, and even in the lives of the most worthy and esteemed people the potential horrors of our fallen natures are all present. Who is virtuous in a visible set of acts may well be vicious in hidden or less noteworthy dimensions of life. This is a phenomenon of humanity which should temper the inclination, which is alive now as ever it was, to demonize criminals. People who murder, or commit dreadful sexual offences, or perpetrate atrocities in situations of conflict, or whatever, are not a separate species of being. They are most likely to be just like us; their lives, however, at some moment are inexorably caught up in situations where ordinary human weakness escapes restraint. Only a very few would seem to be truly pathological criminals; most convicted of crime in our society are normal human beings whose lives have placed them where circumstance betrays morality. There are more criminals than in the past not because of some great moral collapse in society but because the law is, in our day, being extended into increasingly more precise details of daily living, and so criminalizing actions which once were regarded as acceptable, if regrettable. It is the goalposts of the public sense of proper behaviour which are changing. A bloody affray outside a pub, which thirty years ago would have broken up without further action, today results in custodial sentences. In a sanctimonious society of moralists like ours the demonizing of others is always a popular option.

Christians, however, are taught to love their neighbour as themselves, and that includes the rapist, the child molester, and the murderer. Their sins are no worse than many that all of us commit all the time in acts of cruelty and vindictiveness, of jealousy and envy – acts which are not punishable in the courts. But they are acts which are as deeply corrosive to the ideals of an ordered society as if they were. Hidden from public view, and unremarkable because of their awful frequency, the daily sinfulness of men and women, of all of us, is what actually describes human life. What we need is forgiveness, not punishment of others; and that is precisely what the religion of Jesus offers.

Thirty Seven

Passing enthusiasms

୨୦୯ଓ

In the 1960s and 1970s Church leaders identified the essence of Christianity as the pursuit of social justice. The political context of the times was suffused with a radical idealism inspired by the liberation movements against colonialism and what was thought of as economic imperialism by Western corporations in the developing world, by protests against the war in Vietnam, by romantic cults attaching to Mao and to Guevara, and by the pervasive sense that traditional values were collapsing. Sometimes the sense of social protest was tinged with Marxism; where it was not it owed, nonetheless, a considerable debt to the radical *chic* inclination to regard the politics of the Left as peculiarly virtuous and the politics of the Right as somehow rather disgraceful. The Churches breathed in large amounts of the heady atmosphere, and although they stopped short of actually claiming political labels the general tone and direction of their pronouncements on social issues, and the language in which they were rendered, were unmistakably sympathetic. At its most formal the Christian critique issued in a crypto-Marxist assemblage of revolutionary verbiage known as 'Liberation Theology', which is still taught in theological colleges to this day. Its less structured expressions were declaimed from thousands of pulpits. Two agencies of the World Council of Churches announced that Castro's Cuba was the country where the Gospel of Christ was being most faithfully put into practice; in England the General Synod passed a resolution welcoming the closed shop as a Christian model for industrial relations.

What has happened to it all? The simple answer is that secular enthusiasms have changed, and the Christian leadership has followed. Now it has always been true that the Church is locked into a dialectical relationship with the world, and that its views on worldly matters are influenced by prevailing opinion. But in the past there was a key difference; then the political and moral culture which determined the worldly order were themselves fashioned by men who were Christian believers. There was no separation of the sacred and the secular; society was envisaged as a single expression of the divine order upon the earth – straining upwards to an eternal company. It was a scheme which does not, it need hardly be said, correspond with Western society at the end of the second millennium. Change in modern society is also much more rapid than in the past, and there is accordingly less stability in political and moral ideals. The fate of society and how it should be governed are no longer planned in relation to religious values. Christian leaders today, in consequence, should be particularly conscious of the need to perform their tasks of prophetic judgement circumspectly, and to be cautious in identifying the Faith – the very body of Christ in the world – with transient enthusiasms. This is especially so now that it is enthusiasm for Humanity – defined in terms of material needs – which is at the centre of the idealism of the age. Unhappily, Christians seem only too ready to accept Humanity at its own valuation, and to re-define the essence of Christ's message accordingly. The result is the consecretion of 'the caring society', and the acceptance of mere human material welfare as the greatest good that can be imagined.

Thirty Eight

___

Christmas cheer

ഔറ

Christmas is a time for giving. God's gift of his son is echoed in our giving tokens of our affection or regard to those whom we love or know. But it is a transaction: we also receive. And that makes the simple exchange a more complicated matter than it at first appears. For to be a good receiver requires self-conscious understanding. In today's society people – most people, at any rate in Western society – possess so much, and expect so much, that receiving has become routinized. We have lost a sense of gratitude for much that we receive, taking for granted benefits and possessions which in former conditions of society, and in many parts of the developing world now, would be regarded with awe. Jesus commended the poor who give all that they have. Like the lost sheep and the lost coin in the parables, he was reminding us that the value in giving and in receiving is not defined by worldly estimates but by cost in relation to the people involved. The virtue of giving requires the reciprocation of receiving. Consider how this otherwise rather trite observation actually works in reality. Most gifts we make to others are not actual objects, like a toy to a child; they are gifts of time and emotional engagement. We bother with another person in some moment when they are experiencing stress or disappointment in circumstances that are often undramatic, often seemingly trivial. But it is a gift nonetheless, and one which many of us do not bother to make when we have the opportunity to do so. Receiving such commonplace gifts needs awareness on our part, too. We should not take the attentions or kindnesses of others for granted.

Christmas is about the gift of God's love: God so loved the world that he *gave* his only begotten son. That, too, requires our response. We must know how to receive that love. The teaching of Jesus himself is clear; we can show that we have received God's love by loving one another. But what does that mean in daily life? The fact is that humans are fallen creatures, often with extremely vile characteristics. The supremacy of God's love enfolds men and women, but how can *we* rise to such sublime heights? Loving your neighbours is all very well when they seem agreeable; what happens, however, when they are (as humans all are) feckless, mean-minded, faithless? That is precisely where the Christian religion is seen to be an affair not of sentiment and emotional indulgence but as what it truly is – a painful discipline which goes against the grain of our self-seeking. Everyone can love a saint, but it takes a saint to love a sinner. In Christ's religion, however, everyone can become a saint, and that, also, is celebrated at Christmas time. For the first witnesses of God's gift were all kinds of people: simple shepherds in the fields, who left their flocks to find the child in the manger; and wise men who gave up their expectations of majesty to acknowledge the King whose birth was shadowed by a crown of thorns. Giving and receiving: God's gift conveyed in our hands.

Thirty Nine

The Kingdom of Heaven is at hand

ೞೞ

It is the beginning of Holy Week, when Christians, even more than at other times, remember that it is *their* sins which caused the sufferings and death of Jesus. Here is the central mystery in the Christian understanding of God: not the miracle of the Incarnation, not the splendour of Christ's earthly ministry, not even the majesty of the Resurrection – but that the Creator of all things should bother with people like us. Human sin is not an accidental by-product of the way we live, or the consequence of wrong social conditioning. Neither is it the disregard of moral obligations which men and women have over time delivered in response to their desires. Sin is inseparable from our natures, and it issues from faults in ourselves which we cannot put right through our own efforts. Christianity recognizes this. It is not a religion for those who seek to reconstruct a perfect version of humanity, purged of evil and in control of its own destiny. It regards such utopianism – widely implicit in modern attitudes to the capacity of humans to order their own affairs – as simply unrealistic. Christianity is about forgiveness. God forgives human sin. If we reach out to him he will forgive each one of us: the formally virtuous, the depraved, the morally unlovely, the despairing. There is no tariff for our sins; the gift of forgiveness is free. Since no one deserves forgiveness, and no one has even the beginnings of the means of self-correction, the sacrifice of Christ is wholly a gift, the most perfect gift the world will ever know. Holy Week is a good time to devote a moment of reflection on each of its days to recollect our own catalogue of personal sin. When he was in the world Jesus spoke most about the need for men and women to repent. But modern people do not feel the need for repentance. For this is an age of self-esteem, when people dwell upon their rights and exult in their moral freedom; when even religion is embraced as a means of achieving individual emotional benefits, as a kind of therapy, rather than as an act of surrender to the sovereign demands of God. It is hard for those to repent who do not believe they are corrupted. Holy Week, therefore, is also a time of sorrow. The sins of the world lie grimly around us, their evidence never further away than our own actions and neglects. The priceless gift of life, taken for granted, becomes a desert of wastes, as the lost opportunities stack up, and the light handed to us by Christ grows dim in our keeping. What greater sorrow can there be than to realize that it was *our* sins which produced the death of Christ? Yet what more serene happiness is there than the receipt of the forgiveness which the same Christ holds out to those who repent?

The whole concept of repentance needs fresh representation in this generation. The disasters which interrupt the human love of security and material welfare, and which formerly reduced men and women to contrition, no longer do so. Today, in contrast, it is not the awesome presence of God which people see in catastrophe: indeed, virtually any kind of affliction is now taken as evidence there can be no God at all. People cannot imagine a being who could possibly 'allow' human suffering. What vanity! We are now a people who make their own sense of the Divine dependent upon the maintenance of their material well-being. Holy Week is truly a time for reflection on the horror of our own natures.

Forty

Ruler of the heart

ॐ

Two of the most common misunderstandings of the Christian Faith are sadly to be found as much among those inside as among those outside the Church. They are the reduction of religion to a mere set of ethical principles, and the supposition that religious belief is founded upon personal emotional need. Both attitudes humanize the faith, converting it into an extension of the desire which men and women have to achieve a life on earth which is safe and satisfying. Yet at the heart of the message of Jesus is the dreadful fact of human sin. The world of his day was filled with wonderful ethical systems – some of them, indeed, like the Greek pursuit of a balanced social order, achieving the highest thought. But individual lives were still imprisoned in sin. The ethics taught by Jesus comprised measures which gave content to the spiritual life, and they were entirely dependent upon it. The ethics of Jesus were not, there-fore, the centre of his teaching – which was to do with an intrinsic disorder in human life. His great gift to humanity was not an ethical system but personal forgiveness to those who repent. Christianity is a religion of obedience to the divine will, and it is designed for a race who are incapable, through ethical systems or legal devices, to regenerate themselves. Those who are forgiven have then the obligation to try to practise the spiritual life by adopting the ethical principles which Jesus taught to illustrate the nature of the Kingdom. No one can earn redemption by *behaviour,* however exalted and well-intentioned. It is not behaviour but *belief* which presages redemption. The gateway to eternal life is discerned by those who recognize their sinfulness and believe in the sovereignty of

God. The gate is narrow and the way is hard. But Christianity is a religion for sinners; those for whom the vision of paradise is opened are often those whom the world scorns because of their poor behaviour. Yet God upholds them, in all their ethical frailty, because of their belief.

The way to redemption is not established in human emotional need either. Just as ethical behaviour tests the faith of believers and gives it content in the world, so aesthetic sensation and emotional satisfaction may accompany faith but is not itself of the substance of faith. We offer the best we can contrive to God when we worship him – in music, words, art and design. But our faith will be empty if it is founded upon these merely human accomplishments. They are also highly relative to time and circumstance. People who give up going to church because 'it did nothing for me' were probably there for the wrong reasons in the first place. Presence in church is an expression of being incorporated into the body of the Lord in the world – it has nothing to do with emotional or aesthetic satisfaction. Religion is not therapy. It is about the rule of God in individual lives. It is extremely hard for modern people to accept the fact of personal sinfulness; and the religion of Christ, which is based on the prior confession of sin, has little appeal in consequence. It is scarcely necessary to look any further to account for the decline in the numbers of those attending church. It would be helpful if Christians themselves sorted out their priorities, and started to realize that the Christ whom they declare to the world is not an emotional impulse but a living Lord.

_____

Forty One

More than a token

ଞୈଓଔ

The Christian life is centred in the Holy Eucharist, the service of blessing and thanksgiving offered to God in perpetuation of the great supper of the Lord before his sacrifice for our sins. It is also called the mass, or 'missa', to indicate that the followers of Christ are being sent out to teach his truth. The Eucharist is thus the authority of the mission of the People of God, a personal and collective participation in the death of Jesus and the mystery of redemption. It is only secondarily, and by contingence, an affair of human fellowship, where believers share bread and wine as a kind of love-feast memorial of Christ – though that is the aspect of the Eucharist which many Christians today emphasize. The truth and authenticity of Christianity, however, do not depend upon the *experience* of faith among believers (which is the essence of Protestantism in its Evangelical representation) but on the succession of teaching derived from those who stand in the tradition of the Apostles. And the Apostles had themselves first received the body of the Lord and handed on the knowledge of his objective presence in the Eucharist. Christians believe that when the priest celebrates the holy rite Christ himself exists among them, as he descends to the earth veiled from human sight in the forms of bread and wine. This is the most solemn moment in Christian worship, the very union of heaven and earth, always to be venerated, never to be received except in awe and unutterable gratitude.

The Holy Eucharist is also the sublime symbol of the communion of the faithful with the greater company of heaven. By submitting to Christ in the world Christians already become citizens of the unseen Kingdom of the blessed, who beckon them to eternity, and safeguard their way. No one who joins the Church of Christ is ever alone. If the world no longer seems to provide companionship or human love – as so many feel – the citizenship of eternity, encountered at the Eucharist, does. To join in the *missa* of Christ is to be integrated with the mysterious presence of a vast society. This may all sound a bit 'churchy', and so it is. Christ did not deliver his truth to a form of words or a written text. Even the sacred books of Scripture bear their authority because selected by the early Church to be received as the Word of God. Christ did not found a school of thought or a philosophical system, as so many teachers of the ancient world did. He entrusted his truth to a people: to us. We are its guardians and interpreters; what human society will know of him is what existing believers convey in their teaching. And there is the core significance of the Holy Eucharist and of the mission of the Church; the Eucharist purchased our redemption and authorizes our truth. We, shamefully, are forever inclined to reduce this priceless gift to mere personal consolation, a means of self-understanding, individual therapy, a celebration of human camaraderie, a beautiful experience. But the message of Jesus is blood and nails, ripping flesh and the execration of the multitude. The Eucharist is not a piece of sentimental drama; it is the actual presence of Christ amongst those he came to save. Happy are those who are called to such a feast.

Forty Two

Moral confusion

ೞಞ

If puritanism may be defined as the regulation by authority of the details of private life then we are indeed living in an age of puritanism. Puritanism is especially evidenced when interventions are justified on moral grounds. Christians today should be worried because the morality being enforced is a rival to their own – though they are usually unaware of this because it bears a resemblance to Christian ethical principle, and is a sort of simulation and replacement of it. Christian leaders, in fact, often identify their faith with many secular provisions which represent themselves as being – and they may actually be – concerned with human welfare. But welfare and Christian morality do not always coincide. A woman may, with considerable public support, regard it as for her welfare that she procures an abortion, but that can hardly be judged welfare for the unborn life which is discarded. Or a person may be 'taken into care' (or seized by the state, to put it more bluntly) when the family deem it an inconvenience to have them around. There are difficult and painful issues of judgement here. But it is certainly unwise to assume that perceived welfare and Christian morality can always be identified as operating in sympathy.

The moral compulsion of the new puritanism is operating within the undefined relativism of 'the plural society': its moral pedigree is left unstated. No one cares to define the moral philosophy of which it is the detailed blueprint. There is simply an assumption that all enlightened people will agree, as if the authority of the new moral puritanism was self-evident – a kind of Natural Law. It is, indeed, possible to put forward such a justification; but this is rarely attempted, and the moral crudity revealed by politicians who try it is not a pretty sight. Like the august structure of 'political correctness', which is the secular catechism of the new puritanism, it is usually described in terms of welfare provision. It is the substitute for religious belief, not its embodiment. To take Christian moral formulations as the basis for public morality, as in the past, is regarded as sectarian, and an affront to those in the nation whose beliefs are not Christian. It is doubtful if in reality the new puritanism has a basis in ethnicity, nor is it democratic. It is the work of a Humanist elite, many of whom are unaware of the real philosophical pedigree of their ideas.

The result, however, is a progressive diminution of the area of individual liberty – whether in the capacity of parents to care for their children without excessive interventions by agencies of the state, or in the ideas about race or gender which individuals may express. The intentions are laudable; the result is a tyranny of opinion. Christians should worry because the space needed for the free adoption of religious ideas and practices is being taken over by the state – usually under the euphemism of 'regulation'. Some of this is probably beneficial and necessary; a lot of it robs the individual of the ability to exercise free moral choice. The creation of totalitarianism is always disturbing, but it is especially disquieting when it occurs without the declaration of an identifiable ideology – which can be attacked by its opponents – and when its moral absolutism is presented as self-evident welfare. Step by step we are passing into the realm of unfreedom, and sadly the Churches are benignly acquiescent. The notion, also, that human wrongdoing can be eliminated by regulatory legislation is simply unrealistic. People are intrinsically flawed. They need the forgiveness of God rather than the strictures of men.

Forty Three

Raised to glory

ಬಿಂಬ

The Ascension of Christ, celebrated by Christians on Thursday was a demonstration of the splendour and supreme authority of God. The risen Christ was then revealed in majesty, time and eternity were joined, the seen and the unseen worlds opened to the gaze of men. Here was Jesus in the light of the heavenly presence, who had illuminated the world and now was drawn to a perfection beyond the world's understanding. The images that can be appreciated by mortals were exceeded by the actual event, as Jesus passed from his humanity to his divinity – always one, and always of transcendent spiritual beauty, as he holds out to the least lovely of his creatures the priceless gift of eternal citizenship. The modern world notably lacks images of splendour, having come to settle for merely human priorities. It is now difficult, within our cultural references, to imagine the intimations of the divine presence; there are no longer splendid courts or exalted rulers whose style simulated on earth projections of supreme authority. Our human accomplishments, often these days falsely described as 'spiritual values' – like art and music – are a mean substitute for the presence of God. Our daily lives, bereft of religious references of the sort which in traditional societies marked the passage of time, are preoccupied with apparent urgencies which, like the thorns in the Parable of the Sower, exclude authentic spiritual formation.

So let us look again at the fact of the Ascension: Christ in majesty. Christians love and obey Jesus not for what he did for them, not even in the gift of redemption. They certainly do not love him because of any 'meaning' he may give to their lives, or any 'uplift' they may suppose they experience. They love him for himself. Jesus is the eternal God; to be known and feared because of his authority as Creator, to be respected as the author of moral law, to be obeyed because humans are his property. But also, and above all, Jesus is to be loved. Earthly love is a shadow of the divine love, and may educate men and women in some of its preliminaries. Earthly love, however, is deceptive and unreliable: it offers paradise yet delivers an ambiguous mixture of exultation and disappointment. Even when it seems stable it has in reality become merely routinized. We like to think that our love of others, or of another, is unconditional – but that is never really so. Our love of God, if it is truly in us, really is without limitation or reservation, as is God's love for us. So greatly did he love the work of his hands – which he had placed in an environment of such hazard and potential sorrow, but where we receive a nurturing in eternal citizenship – that he died for our salvation. If we would see the power of that love we should behold the Christ of the Ascension: the final demonstration of the divine truth that goodness overcomes evil, and that the partial values of the world have their perfection in the Kingdom that is everlasting. Rejoice at being called to know such a Saviour; be amazed that the frailty of our love is met by the supreme love of God.

Forty Four

Wrong perspectives

ಇಂೞ

A young child dies in a house fire; thousands perish in an earth-quake; a virus deprives a young man of his future; a baby is born dead. The question so frequently asked by this generation is 'Can there be a God when such things happen?' The sense that commonplace events like these are an outrage against human entitlements prompts many to scepticism or complete atheism; indeed the apparent arbitrariness of life is probably the chief cause of defection from religious belief today. People suppose their moral instincts about the fate of others – not to speak of themselves – are higher than those of a Divinity who can afflict such horrors upon a race they have been told he loves. The just and the unjust, furthermore, are equally subject to the chances of life. The good and the bad are liable to suffer in balanced numbers. But to question the existence of a benign God on the basis of such evidence – which was equally available to the countless millions of religious believers who have preceded us on the planet – is simply a piece of human vanity. We have too high an estimate of our own value. The moral sense of the modern world is centred in our claims to an existence which is free of suffering; we regard it as unacceptable if our material welfare is not considered the supreme consideration. Thus people today are anchored by authentic materialism: they see themselves as most truly 'spiritual' when they regard the material 'care' of others as more important than the values and beliefs which all of us exist to discover. They love humanity above the love of God. And presumably they also imagine that men and women are so possessed of inherent goodness that they really are entitled to a pain-free existence.

Yet God has willed things differently. The scriptural accounts of the Creation, though symbolical, do lay out great truths. One of these, in a way the most obvious, is that God created the world for his own (and unknowable) purposes, and saw that it was good for those purposes. The world, as part of an exploding universe, is transient and unstable, and the creatures which generated upon its surface are subject to the same processes of chance and change as everything else. Dust you are, God told humanity, and to dust you shall return. The works of God's hands, being creatures and not the Creator, are lesser beings and they are intrinsically flawed. Jesus came into the world not because humanity is good and lovely, and can expect nothing but happiness in life, but because men and women are corrupted in their natures and are unable in their own strengths to achieve amendment. Their lives are *not* their own, but are leased to them for a short term and on explicit conditions. Education in spirituality comes through experience of the world, the good and the evil which happen to men and women comprising the divine curriculum. The earth is a place of trial, not a safe resting place. It is our vanity which produces our yearning for a reality stripped of its content, our sense of self-worth which demands that we shall have whatever we ask. But God is the sovereign of all things, and we are called to trust him. To doubt his providence is a great sin.

Forty Five

The mirror of imperfection

ཐༀ

People are very tiresome. This may be disagreeable to have to confess: but if we ignore reality we shall deceive ourselves. Anyone who is cheerily optimistic about humanity is simply liable to false judgement. People are not very nice. Yet made by God to have a companionship with him, and called by God to be the stewards of the earth, men and women are capable of a kind of greatness; they are disordered versions of perfection. They can imagine moral splendour but cannot deliver it, even in the most trivial aspects of daily life. They are created as spiritual beings, yet their exercise of their spiritual faculties actually becomes a compound of vanity: in place of intimations of celestial values they interpose the individual pursuit of personal significance and the aesthetic sensations derived from human accomplishments. Their concern for the welfare of others, elevated enough in relation to those with whom they are linked by immediate ties of affection, is flawed by self-interest and a curious censoriousness about those whose taste for good works is not commensurate with their own. Human life has dignity, for it is a gift of God. But we as individuals do not. The expressions 'human dignity' and 'the sanctity of human life', when properly used, describe qualities imparted to us by God – qualities we frequently misuse or choose to ignore; they do not describe what we are actually like. God's gift of the dignity of life is entrusted to us for the span of a lifetime: the extent to which we employ it to make ourselves dignified is up to each one of us. The record of accomplishment is not good. Jesus always spoke of humanity as in need of radical change – nothing less than the complete rejection of our corrupted wills, and the attendant wrong priorities, and our submission to the sovereignty of God. Time and time again, however, each one of us makes our own desires the sovereign of our lives. Then our potential for dignity slips away, and our tiresomeness passes into sin.

Yet Jesus did not come into the world to condemn the world, but to offer men and women the prospect of salvation. And there is the authentic dignity of humanity. It is the *gift* of life which is sacred; our lives may be touched by its sanctity through our pursuit of the divine purpose. Instead, we interpret life as a matter of rights and entitlements, with ourselves as the beneficiaries, not of an eternal citizenship, but of immediate worldly rewards: the treasure is stored up on earth. Even so, the eternal splendour flickers dimly in the life of everyone, for Jesus called each one to be his follower. That light will illuminate the whole of ourselves if we submit to God's will. Men and women are not transformed thereby: their corrupted humanity remains – but they are *forgiven*. Self-seeking and greedy, an unhappy affliction to others and an habitué of sin: people are nevertheless the raw materials of the Kingdom of Christ. First, we must rid ourselves of false sentimentality about humanity. We are not very satisfactory; we are given to wickedness; we embrace wrong priorities. Modern society, when all the Humanist euphemisms are discarded, is shabbily unacquainted with the pursuit of higher purposes – a projection of the inherent human craving to settle for material rather than spiritual goals. Yet look into the face of another and you will see the face of Christ: a face of sorrow, awaiting the act of contrition which restores dignity. This is the indwelling Christ, who awaits recognition by us – so great is his patience and his love.

Forty Six

Clear advice

ଧⴰℭଷ

It is quite rare these days to hear a sermon about sexual morality.
This is extraordinary since we live at a time when sex is
exhibited in so many public ways – in television dramas and
discussions, in advertising, in school programmes of 'moral'
teaching. The agenda for debate of human sexuality is set by the
media, and it is thoroughly secularized; the clergy appear to
follow its main lines in such advice as they do offer. It is the
secular moralists, medical experts, and the hosts of care workers
who define the various issues. The Church of the past was
not silent on these matters, nor is the Catholic Church today –
despite the apparent rejection of its teaching by so many of
its lay adherents, claiming a right to 'think for themselves'.
The pulpits of the Victorian era we imagine to have been
thunderously precise in declamations about sexual morality,
though later caricatures, serving later inclinations to simplify
the past, cloud judgement of the matter. How is it possible to
account for the reticence of the Church of England of today?
Why do the preachers opt for discourses about Third World
poverty rather than the rules of sexuality? Sex, after all, involves
the most familiar forms in which individuals encounter moral
choice. The answer probably lies in a horror of controversy.
Church leaders abhor any rocking of the boat. Yet virtually
everything which is intellectually serious provokes dispute, so
everything is controversial. There is also a paradox: progressive
choice in sexual morality falls within an acceptable liberal consensus, whereas 'traditional' teaching is perceived to be controversial unless it can be firmly identified as 'family values'. The
teaching of Jesus was divisive; he did not set out to establish a

consensus and spoke of his truth as bringing a sword – and that brother would be divided against brother. There is no intellectual advance without the testing of propositions, and in the process the boat is rocked all the time. If the Church would fulfil its prophetic calling it should give up avoiding controversy. The leaders are delighted with themselves when they risk incurring unpopularity, as they suppose, by supporting the claims to social justice of various groups: so why can't they say something clear, if unpopular, about abortion?

Now human sexuality is a controversial area precisely because there have been great advances of knowledge. Some practices once considered vile are now, because shown to be built into people by conditions over which they have no control, correctly considered acceptable. Some sexual impulsions, long judged vile, are always vile: adultery, for example, or sex with animals. In some matters technology has intervened, and a whole secondary realm of moral ambiguity has opened up. Difficult decisions are needed: but often the leaders of the Protestant Churches simply decline to give a lead, even to their own followers. How many people know that the Church of England, in its formal teaching, condemns both divorce and abortion? They rarely hear those matters taught in the pulpit except as open 'issues' about which there is current public debate – thus, once again, implicitly accepting the validity of the secular moral agenda. Church leaders have a duty to advise their own Church members about the law of the Church, and to make sure that they have got it clear themselves. They also have a duty to assist in extending modern knowledge about human sexuality. The two are not incompatible.

Forty Seven

———

Religious loyalty

80C3

People today seem to make their choices about religious belief – or the abandonment of it, in so many cases – on the basis of personal need rather than considered reflection on the nature of religious traditions. This in itself indicates a view of religion which is defective: that its purpose is individual sustenance. Christians have always held that their religion is true in itself; that it expresses a set of obligations towards the Creator of all things, who had made himself known to his creatures through a series of very specific requirements, and that the Faith itself involved at its centre the abandonment of personal claims in order to achieve a surrender to the priorities set by God. It is the sacrificial element in personal religious belief which is absent in modern responses. Men and women look for individual fulfilment when they make their choices. Choice itself, of course, is a relatively modern feature of religious subscription. For in most traditional societies religion was espoused collectively; it was a matter of identity and loyalty – not a question of individual emotional satisfaction. This was a problem for the early Church. In the Greek and Roman worlds individuals could adopt all kinds of religious cultic practices, but they were only allowed to do so provided they retained a simultaneous civic allegiance to whatever officially sanctioned religion prevailed. This even operated, through the Roman practice of indirect rule, amongst the Jewish populations of Palestine and the dispersed Jewish peoples of the Mediterranean coasts. The first Christians broke with this convention, and were periodically persecuted by authority as a consequence. But with the accession of the Church to official recognition, and its incorporation into the political order, Christians too adopted the prevalent mode of regarding religious allegiance as an indication of public obligation and civic identity. This is inevitably the way with sacral values: the modern world excludes from proper membership of society those whom it considers as enemies of the prevailing virtues – racists, for example, or those with unapproved sexual proclivities.

So making choices about religious belief is actually something of an unusual privilege, in the wider perspective. In our case it derives from the general privatizing and individualizing of faith. But this ought to increase, rather than diminish, the seriousness with which the aspirant to faith scrutinizes and learns religious tradition. And here is the great problem. For people today do *not* study religious ideas in any systematic fashion; instead they are eclectic and random, picking up information through chance, and applying it to individual requirements rather than asking if the ideas they encounter are true in themselves. God exists independently of our needs, and the universe was not created in order to fulfil them. An enquiry into religion which derives from a personal desire for individual significance – which inspires most religious reflection today – is of all things the least likely to arrive at truth. It will arrive, instead, at a distorted mirror image of each person's demands. What then happens is the sad experience of the world today: men and women make up their own religious systems for themselves, and are bitterly disappointed when the institutional Church does not appear to be in correspondence with them.

Forty Eight

What do we remember?

ℰℬℭℬ

The sacrificial core of the Christian life, like so much else, is now generally understood by Christians themselves in a social or collective sense. People are exhorted to make sacrifices of time or of resources in order to redress imbalances in the use of the earth's resources, or to care for the well-being of others, or to secure justice in human relationships. These are all very laudable ends. But Christian sacrifice should have personal spiritual formation as its primary purpose, and although that certainly involves such wider issues, and their implications for the political and social order – and may indeed be a school for spiritual education – the first priority in sacrificial living must always be a consequence of surrendering to God things which would otherwise bring us pleasure or advantage. Spiritual formation begins with acknowledgement of sin, and sin derives from the pursuit of benefits. Our lives were not given to us in order that we expend them in comfort and security, but so that we might discover the will of our Creator. Suffering is annexed to this, since as fallen creatures our inclinations are to seek material advantages and emotional satisfaction. Christ, however, called his followers to leave even family and friends for his sake. It is the things we don't want to do which are likely to prove the ones which educate the soul, and the advantages we forego, by act of will rather than by the chance of circumstance, which cultivate within our beings the authentic characteristics of a citizen of eternity. Sacrificial living is marked by the offering of time: life seems to call us to so many activities, yet the call of Christ is to prayer and the spaciousness of listening to God.

Remembering those who have died in warfare is a moment of true sacrifice – the sacrifice of lives is reproduced, in a small way, in the sacrifice of time to evoke the memory of the dead. The fallen of all conflicts are included; the sea of faces returns to life in the recollection of survivors. There is, however, even in this act of apparent nobility, an unwelcome intrusion of self-regard. For the act of remembrance now frequently expresses a culture of nostalgia: the dead are remembered in a haze of recalled memories, the reassembly of a world we have lost. It is unavoidable but needs conscious control; otherwise it is not the sacrifice of the fallen which is remembered but our own past lives. Herein lies the renewed popularity of Remembrance Sunday, and the recent revival of Armistice Day observance. Military valour and the glory of conflict are not modern virtues, at least in the Western world, and the increased emphasis placed upon Remembrance in the past few years derives in part from the efforts of a generation of war veterans who are aware that they are themselves passing from the scene, and partly from nostalgic recollection of the golden days of former decades. Nostalgia may be a virtue, in that it can root us in the past and so provide a continuity in personal and collective awareness of our values. But it may also rob the present of purpose, if it fails to use the past to offer lessons. For Christians the essential lesson is the centrality of sacrifice, and the pursuit of truth above the advantage of the individual.

Forty Nine

———

A universal truth

ℬℭ

Scientific discovery and modern intellectual culture have largely demystified everything. We no longer expect the world to be moved by hidden forces, or individual lives to be directed by supernatural agencies. An active belief in direct interventions by mysterious presences has now, at least in Western understanding, moved to the fringe – to New Age religion, perhaps, or to a dubious popular penchant for astrology and similar absurd diversions. Religion itself has, by some, come to be seen as merely a human phenomenon; an invention of a race eager to secure its own significance in the universal scheme of things; the misunderstanding of preceding generations who lacked our capability to account for the mechanics of existence; the social control exercised by primitive societies.

Yet an authentic religious interpretation of the world was never dependent on a God who worked by magic. In the Judaic-Christian tradition God was disclosed through his Creation, through the very materiality of things. The world was not an illusion, and it was not directed by mysterious forces – but by forces for which an explanation was not at the time available. The universe expressed a great act of creative will, and the Creator himself was not an arbitrary and unknowable force, an anonymous First Cause, but the one who operated through laws which he had set up. It is those laws which disclose the nature of the Creation (through not its purpose) which scientific advance enables us to begin to understand. The intellectual culture we then assemble in order to explain it, on the other hand, is very much a human invention. And there is a modern dilemma. Humanity is called by God to take part with him in the creative process, and to develop the planet entrusted to our stewardship, and to use his gift of life in order to be, as the Bible says, 'fruitful'. Yet humanity remains imperfect, a collection of creatures separated from the fullness which attaches only to the Creator. Hence the imperfections of the intellectual culture, and, above all, the pervasive modern sense that discoveries about the laws of the Creation have somehow removed the need to believe in a Creator. In fact the demystification of reality is an enormous advantage. For humanity was always mistaken to suppose that God worked by magic: such primitivism, like the sacrifice of animals upon altars, has been superseded by the divine gift of a progressive understanding. Men and women have been invited by the Creator to probe the nature of reality, and in doing so have begun to define both themselves and the very substance of their material environment. Nothing explains itself, however, and knowing how the laws of creation work does not present the observer with philosophical interpretation. God is not known about by magical effusions, but by the unfolding accumulation of evidences of his presence in the things he has made – and that is the nature of religious tradition. Good and bad interpretations are found together in all this – like the wheat and the tares – and it is our duty as reflective creatures to separate them. The Christian life, therefore, is active intellectually, as each one of us seeks to achieve a culture of understanding which glories in a God not of magic but of true revelation. The universe itself is his handiwork.

Fifty

Listening to God

ℰᏅᏣᎶ

Enormous members of people pray; far more than go to the church or even regard themselves as religious in any formal sense. It used to be said, during the Second World War, that there were no atheists in a foxhole. Resort to prayer is not an indication of any inherent characteristic of humanity, however, except possibly an indication of desperation in conditions of fear. It probably indicates the early conditioning of the individual, remembered practice from early childhood dredged up by later crisis. Prayer in these conditions, like the prayers which form in even the least spiritually developed people in times of need, are requests. They are petitionary exhortations for God to save them from certain calamities or give them specified benefits. God is merciful, and will always listen, especially when his creatures are suffering. The God who came into the world as Christ, and himself died in a great act of expiation for human sin, is never going to be inattentive when his children call out to him for help. And prayer is always answered – though in God's wisdom and not in the immediate concession of human demands. We are called to suffering in the world; it is a place of tribulation where men and women are educated in spirituality and discover the contours of reality. What we would ask for ourselves is not often – is not usually – what is spiritually beneficial. Prayers which merely define our needs, furthermore, have a tendency never to develop through life, except to the extent that our needs change in nature. So prayer is often a childlike cry for help. It may be none the worse for that: it is as little children, Jesus told us, that we are called to enter the Kingdom of Heaven. But such prayer will plainly be one-dimensional.

When Jesus went into the desert places to pray, and gave to humanity the supreme example of prayer, and when he taught his followers the prayer which bears his name, it was the acclamation of God's greatness which preceded any request. That is what the prayers of those who pray only in need lack. For the greatness of God far exceeds our imagination, and the best prayer, in consequence, exists when we seek to empty our minds of the priorities of our daily lives and to create the interior space and silence in which we can listen for his voice. The less clutter the better. Because we can only experience reality in the vocabulary and symbols of the world, God will appear to us in sanctified sequences of familiar earthly images. The earth is the Lord's, and he created it in a fashion which would sustain human life; it also, as a result, bears the token and semblance of those attributes of himself which he wishes to convey to us. Above all, by becoming himself a man in the person of Christ, God irradiated the world of our experience with the divine presence. When we create space and silence in ourselves, through the dynamics of prayer, we hear again the voice of the Saviour as surely as they heard it who gathered on the shores of Galilee and in the desert of Judea. The truth about prayer, like the truth about the Christian life in general, is that people simply do not try to put it into effect. Listening to God is half of the process of spiritual growth; the other half is learning the religious tradition in which he is conveyed, so that his voice can be recognized.

Fifty One

The language of praise

ℬ☙☚

Worship is a difficult subject for modern people. The forms still in use in the Churches derive from the kind of ritualized honour paid to political superiors in the ancient world: acclamations of greatness and power, expressed in verbal images which evoke a world of autocracy which no longer exists, at least among peoples of the West. The petty potentates who provided the original models expected their subjects to address them in precisely the same styles as were commonly used to address God. Hence the ease with which the people of Israel could recognize a Covenant between themselves and their God: it was just like the treaties made between kings and between local sovereigns and their nobility, to secure allegiance and to guarantee the performance of specified services. Two such minor autocrats are still remembered publicly in the liturgical use of the Church of England. Sehon, King of the Amorites, and Og, the King of Bashan, succumbed to Israeli expansionism, and, amazingly, their names, through the recitation of the psalms, are said aloud in church to this day – surviving even the revisionism of the modern era. But most people in the modern era do not really find it satisfactory to render their obedience to God in terms of ancient political submission. And the models of present political authority are equally unsuitable. God does not govern the universe through populist democracy. Yet God is sovereign, and when humans forget it their spirituality withers.

It is necessary, similarly, for each of us to worship God in order to maintain control of the person. God is the sovereign of individual lives, and worship is the means by which we acknowledge it. This is not only a matter of public witness; worship is also undertaken in private, and then it is a daily submission to the authority of God over the whole of our being. Our desires, and our priorities, are constantly slipping out of the control we have the foolishness to suppose we can exercise over them. Worship recalls us to the reality of our natures. Our passions are forever achieving ascendancy over our reasoned wills. Worship reminds us that we are subjects and not masters, and that our baser instincts are not merely marginal visitors to our psyche but are near to its centre.

What forms of words, then, and what kinds of symbolical acts are suited to worship at the start of the new millennium? Certainly something of the traditional uses is important – even crucial. For we are rooted in the Christian past; ours is a religion which we receive within a tradition of believers, and on whose authority we know it to be true. To employ the uses they used, and to express ourselves, still, in the rhetoric they fashioned is a means of self-identity, and an actual participation in a universal and eternal society. Liturgy, in this sense, is something that has to be learned; like Christian truth itself, it is not just picked up from the current environment. Yet we need also to be inventive to use the appropriate images of our own times to approach God and to acknowledge his power. This is more difficult than in the past, for the modern world lacks acquaintance with the majestic and the serene. But God himself approaches those who seek to approach him: knock, and the door will be opened, with Christ to light the way.

Fifty Two

Hail to the Lord's anointed

⍟

On Palm Sunday, which is tomorrow, Christians remember the descent of Christ from the Mount of Olives, riding on the humblest of beasts, yet greeted by the exultant crowds as King. Thereafter he ascended the Mount Zion, and the Temple Mount, for the last acts of his ministry on earth, his farewell to his faithful disciples, and his death. It was a sacred drama without parallel; a self-sacrifice which bestowed forgiveness to a people whose dreadful sins had caused it. And there, precisely, is the reason why Christians, then as now, are exultant. For Christ the King did not promise a transformation of life on earth, or the resolution of human moral frailty, or the perfection of our natures. He did not come for a people who deserved any amelioration of their horrific propensity to behave as creatures with lower natures – who yet could imagine the splendour of the immortality to which they were called. Christ came upon an ass: he addressed the most debased of his human subjects, those who before were without hope, the destitute in spirit, those whose weaknesses were despised by the world and whose prospects were, in worldly terms, extremely bleak. He came for sinners; and it is all those who recognize that they *are* sinners who receive from him the crown of everlasting glory. He bestows it on the vilest criminal, like the thief who was crucified with him, or like the outcast sex offenders hounded by the popular press today: the only qualification for entry into Christ's Kingdom is personal acceptance of the sovereignty of Christ, and the confession of sins. The Kingdom of Heaven consists of those who are forgiven; Christianity is the company not of the righteous or the pious or the morally correct, but of those who try to love God.

This Kingdom, therefore, is open to everyone. You do not have to achieve special understanding, and Jesus himself said that it was with the simplicity of little children that men and women are called to enter his Kingdom. You do not need to achieve moral purity: you need only to strive to make your trusteeship of your body, and your relations with others, more approximate to the ideal imagined by those who are to be bearers of Christ in the world. In the stark desert places of Judea, and amidst the elegiac landscapes of Galilee, Christ called people of all sorts and abilities to respond to his welcome. For it is men and women who are now his body on earth, frail witnesses to truths beyond their easy comprehension and yet the human agents of eternal salvation. It is probably the sinfulness of Christians themselves which most puts people off the Church; they see how little membership of Christ's body seems to affect corrupted natures. And so it is – the glory of the Church. Christ's true body in the world is made up of those who are really of the world, who share the world's appalling imperfections and whose liability to sin attaches to them despite their efforts. It cannot be repeated too frequently: the Christian Church is for sinners. It is the company of those who are forgiven. All we are asked to do to enter such splendour is to stand, where they stood, in submission, on the side of the Mount of Olives, and to confess that 'blessed is he who comes in the name of the Lord'. The great love of God comes to us a free gift; we have only to reach out to the welcoming arms of the Saviour.

Fifty Three

The authority of truth

෨ඏ

It is becoming common for government agencies and media pundits to refer to different religious bodies as 'Faith Communities' – as if 'faith' was a sort of agreed view of the world which for ethnic or historical reasons has developed according to independent traditions of understanding. This assessment is hugely encouraged by broadcast magazine programmes in which all the different religious groups are accorded a practical equality, and by the presentation of the world religions, side by side, in school curriculae. Modern opinion runs strongly in favour of all this sort of thing. In general, astonishingly ill-informed about religion – and especially about the Christian religion – it supposes that the different faiths merely reflect a shared human inclination to posit the existence of a Creator, and regards the form this takes as simply a matter of past cultural conditioning. Thus Islam, Judaism, Christianity, Hinduism, and Buddhism indicate different dimensions of a single phenomenon: the human aspiration to account for the nature of reality. The emphasis here is on *human*, for religion is conceived, according to this style of evaluation, as a catering for some kind of human need. If religious belief is generalized enough, and if its actual doctrines are subordinated to the supervening priority of human material need, then it is quite possible to conclude, as many now do, that there is no major difference between the religions. Indeed, a past emphasis on their actual doctrinal contents is now judged to have inspired warfare, social dislocation, and conflict. As usual, the progressive views of the age are well represented inside the Christian Churches, and the proposals for inter-faith services are being ever more insistently brought forward. There are reasons why they should be resisted.

Christianity is not a sequence of emotional impressions but a clear structure of doctrine. In the person of Jesus it was God himself who was in the world, and his words and teaching, therefore, are not susceptible to correction or re-evaluation in the light of any other religious tradition. Ours is not the first age in which the Judaic-Christian body of religious ideas has been acquainted with other religions: Psalm 69 declares emphatically that 'the gods of the nations are idols every one', and throughout Christian history there has been a knowledge of the religious practices of Greece and Rome. The Church itself has always held that a knowledge of God is indeed present to other world religions, but that it is derived from natural religion and is therefore latent and descriptive knowledge, and is defective because necessarily partial. To treat all religions as a parity is in itself to cultivate relativity of understanding. And who is to decide which of the religious ideas and practices of humanity are acceptable and which are not? What of the human sacrifices practised in the pre-Colombian religions of Latin America – religions now romanticized in television documentaries? What of the immolation of wives on funeral pyres practised in Hindu society before abolition as a result of contact with Western ideas? All religions are not the same – unless they are reduced to statements which are so general that they become merely abbreviations of human claims to significance. Mutual respect between the 'Faith Communities' is plainly desirable; disinclination to recognize their huge difference is not.

Fifty Four

Counting the days

Human longevity has advanced at exactly the same time that the decay of religious belief in the West has left many people perplexed about the purpose of human life. People are living longer, but to what end? If the purpose of life is indeed, as many appear to declaim, the pursuit of happiness then there is a certain formal logic in desiring to live longer. But it is also to ignore the often horrific realities of old age: loss of mobility, dependence on others, social marginalization, and, above all, a melancholy and pervasive sense of loss. Living longer is actually compulsory. Relatives conspire with the medical profession – who are terrified of having lawsuits brought against them unless they use every available technological trick to keep the elderly alive – to prolong life, whatever its quality. The old themselves have an understandable curiosity about how things will turn out; survival, for them, may offer the prospect of knowing how the next instalment of a television drama may unfold. Thus the trivialities of existence. But how many want to stay alive in order to enrich an understanding of reality itself, or to explore still further the mysteries of religious truth? Not, one suspects, very many. People are living longer, and the extra years are expended in a gentle but inconsequential pursuit of something to do until the end comes. Human life retains a low purpose for those who all along supposed its purpose was gratification of the senses and the exploration of human relationships, or whose highest aspiration was described by attempts to attend to the material welfare of other people. For those for whom the purpose of life is a preparation for eternity, however, it is the spiritual quality of an individual existence, and not its length, which is decisive.

Life a gift of God. It is not to be treated, by Christians at any rate, as if it was at the disposal of the individual recipient. Nor should the chance of life for others be decided according to the requirements individuals set for themselves. Thus the number of children born into the world should not be determined by what adverse effect their nurture may have on the living standards or leisure opportunities of their parents – nor yet by the insistent modern rationalization that the numbers of children should be determined by the capacity of the parents to rear them in material conditions which are arbitrarily fixed according to the bourgeois models of Western households.

Christians believe that life is entrusted to us in order that we use our time on earth as an education of the spiritual person. This is not necessarily a cerebral exercise: God calls the whole of his human creation to share with him in developing the glory of the Creation, and Jesus said explicitly that those who would enter the Kingdom of Heaven should be like little children. Salvation is the distillation of life's experiences into a simple act of assent to the sovereignty of God. That is also the way to regard the additional years which modern longevity is delivering. Enrichment then means a growth in poverty of human expectations, and the joy of a long life is that it is one which is fashioning us for eternity.

Fifty Five

The truth of the Spirit

ಬಂಡ

How it is possible to determine which version of Christian truth is authentic to the teaching of Christ and which is not? For Christians have differed among themselves about the meaning and authority of the Faith from the very beginning: witness the exhortations to uniformity of teaching in the letters of St Paul. Is there, indeed, a single body of truth at all, or is there, as modern Anglicans sometimes imagine, a kind of 'dispersed authority' which encompasses varied interpretations, so that the core message of Christ only emerges through a series of conflicting exchanges and over time? This last is unlikely, since the Church of Christ is literally his body in the world: it is Christ himself who presides over the People of God. His earthly representatives are not capable of being in error when they are declaring the nature of his authority. The declaration of Christian truth has by definition to be infallible when it relates to the nature of God and the salvific work procured in the ministry of Christ – both when he was directly in the world, and subsequently when he was in it, no less authoritatively, in his Church. The first test of the authenticity of Christian truth is that it is declared by the *whole* People of God; there can be no such thing as a 'separated' or a 'national' Church, since Christ is universal, and the means of determining his will is universal also. In the history of the Church the continuing revelation of the divine will has been made by representatives from the entire world gathering in council. What they declare as the mind of Christ is in fact what Christ wills, and cannot possibly be any other, since they *are* in a sense Christ, his very body, entrusted with the commission given by Christ and sent out by him to teach all nations. The authority of Christian truth is not found in resort to its origins, in an attempt (now particularly popular among modern liberal scholars, and those with reasons to relativize religious understanding) to 'discover' the original practices or intentions of the first adherents. Nor does the authority of the Church derive from the Bible – whose composition, in fact, was determined by the Church itself, and was intended to furnish *proofs* of what the Church was teaching, not its first source. The authority of Christian truth lies in the consensus of the faithful, gathered from the whole body of believers. The religion of Jesus is dynamic; its dialectical exchanges with the historical and cultural and social shifts, and its prophetic insistence on discerning permanent truths in the transience of the continuing change all round it, convey the knowledge of a Christ whose will is what the People of God declare it to be – for they are his mouthpiece. That is the astonishing authority of Christian truth: that certainty is entrusted to flawed and sinful creatures, who yet declare a splendour to which they are called, and whose anticipations of eternity are available to the humblest understanding.

At Whitsun the Church celebrates God the Holy Spirit. How can they be certain that they are protected in all truth? It is because the Spirit, in the assurance of Jesus himself, will guide them into it. Individual believers may produce false or distorted interpretations, but the People of God collectively can never depart from the authentic message. They may at times have influence among the societies of humanity; they may, however, be a small company in other moments of history. But they will always speak as the voice of Christ himself.

Fifty Six

The Holy Trinity

෨〇෪

We are fortunate to be alive at a time of such spectacular advances in knowledge of the universe. The Book of Genesis had described the earth and the stars as made out of nothing. and the life of humanity as being on unstable moment between Creation and the inevitable extinction of everything – described, in biblical images (not inaccurately, in all probability), in terms of fire. There are references in scriptural texts to rocks falling from the heavens; and in his prediction of the end Our Lord himself referred to the sun being darkened, the moon ceasing to give light, and the stars falling from the skies. Christianity has, accordingly, always taught that the lives of men and women comprise a temporary state of affairs: the universe will expire and living things with it. Time therefore is precious; there is a limited span in each life, and in the life of the whole race, before judgement. Some religions had taught a kind of stable state within which human life was set, and some a condition of eternal recurrence, so that lives were recycled and points of reference returned time and time again. But in the Judaic-Christian understanding God has a will for each person, and each person's life is integrated with a cosmic drama which has a catastrophic ending. The majestic scale of this sequence is still beyond human comprehension: the beginnings of a coherent interpretation are starting in our day, however, and they indicate that the creative power of God considerably exceeds the limited vision of preceding generations.

God can only be known about by us from a finite perspective. Modern knowledge of the universe suggests that the numbers of such perspectives are astonishingly great. Our perspective is the earth, and all we can know about God derives from the images which are earthly in origin – and which we are now applying in order to interpret the heavens. In the process that will become changed, just as our anticipations of the creative nature of God are expanding. The God of our understanding, however, is a God who has chosen to call us to participate with him in the development of our own planet: the discovery of the nature of the universe is a by-product of the process. Our knowledge of God is not merely latent, however. He has made himself known to us explicitly. God has *revealed* himself, and in Christian understanding this disclosure of his nature included his love for his creatures and his promise of immortality for those who respond to his call to faithfulness. Christians no longer need to imagine God in the abstract categories appropriate to the author of something as diverse as the universe, for they can see him in the person of Jesus. The Creator sent his son into the world to confirm that the primitive intimations of his reality were authentic. He also, and most importantly, came to save them. The Holy Spirit preserves those who respond to God's calling in all essential truth. To observe the scale and diversity of the great explosion which we call the universe is to recognize that God discloses himself in many ways. For his love of humanity he chose three, and it is this Trinity of love which Christians honour and celebrate on Sunday. 'Thou deckest thyself with light as it were with a garment: and spreadest out the heavens like a curtain' (Psalm 104). There may be all kinds of other ways in which God is known, which are unavailable to us because of the finite nature of our perspective; but the three ways in which we do see him are all-sufficient for salvation.

Fifty Seven

A modern deception

&)C&

The public are constantly being assured that 'ethical committees' will examine carefully all proposals which might affect the moral status of scientific research. Doubtless the deliberations of these bodies will be careful; but will they be ethical? With issues like the nature and extent of genetical engineering, or the guidelines within which the medical profession should operate when terminating human life, there are indeed puzzling complications, for these are uncharted waters. With matters such as divorce law reform or the moral teaching to be given in schools, there already exists past practice by which the problems of the day may be assessed. But what is the pedigree of the ethical system which the 'ethical committees' will activate, what is its authority, and who is to determine it? There are complications here germane to the assumption, now widely made, that this is a plural society, and that it is the duty of government, and government bodies, to protect the integrity of the moral understanding of the various (and often competing) components of the pluralism. What happens, however, when the moral understanding or practices of particular sections of the pluralism are perceived by government to be morally inadmissible? Thus the law does not look benignly upon the practices of plural marriage and female circumcision, though these receive moral acceptance within some religious groups. And the state itself, even in a plural society, does actually promote its own moral understanding. Thus racism and sexism are discouraged for moral reasons by government. Issues such as abortion or divorce are allowed by the state but are anathema to significant sections of society, and for moral reasons. The Church of

England (the national Church, after all), and the Roman Catholic Church, are opposed to both. Whose morality was it, therefore, which prevailed when abortion and divorce were legalized? The answer is that it was Humanist morality; but since there is no accepted recognition of a Humanist moral system in this country, and since governments do not declare the authority of the morality of their actions – presuming them to be self-evident – the whole area is left undefined. Once the public committees which determined moral considerations always had a token bishop among their membership: even he has now been replaced, in general, by a representative of the social services industry. The continued existence of a national Establishment of religion in this, as in so much else, is a highly formal phenomenon.

The public should decidedly *not* be reassured by the findings of the 'ethical committees'. For all they do, in effect, is to define morality as whatever humans think is beneficial for them. They operate a kind of sliding scale of human self-interest. Thus however immoral a medical proceeding may be, interpreted in the light of a traditional ethical teaching, it becomes acceptable if it can be shown that illnesses can be cured or lives can be lived longer. How the authors of our culture, and the saints and thinkers of the past, would weep to behold such crudity! But our generation actually prides itself on what it considers its moral consciousness.

Fifty Eight

The peace of God

೮ುಛಿ

Christians are greatly given to praying for world peace, or for peace in particular theatres of conflict which happen to have been drawn to their attention by press coverage. What do they think they are asking God to arrange? If all conflict between peoples was produced by uncomplicated self-interest, or by sheer wickedness applied in circumstances of obvious evil, the matter need hardly be raised. But the truth is that most conflicts are extremely complicated, and the appearance that they are not may derive solely from acceptance of the polemical assertions of one party only. Christians often pray for the 'reconciliation' of differences; most conflicts, however, if not caused by serious ideological differences soon have serious issues of principle involved in their purpose. No one, presumably, would now suggest that there should have been 'reconcilation' between the Nazis and the Jews they were subjecting to a Final Solution: these matters of principle and ideology were plainly irreconcilable and righteousness had to be achieved through brute force. Then, surely, it was right to pray for the success of war aims.

In traditional Christian teaching, government exists in societies as God's providential way of allowing humans to cope with the terrible effects of their own corruption. Government was provided because men and women are fallen creatures, who require the coercion which government provides in order to preserve social order. And that order is necessary for people to be able to live the moral life, and to perpetuate society itself in conditions which are not determined by arbitrary forces. Government does not exist because of human genius, therefore, but is an indication of human moral frailty. In reality, of course, people have always differed about how government should conduct its stewardship of the peoples over whom it exercises a measure of control, and in advanced societies these differences have achieved intellectual nobility in sophisticated enquiry about the philosophical basis. This last condition, incidentally, is at a markedly low ebb in modern Western societies – which should cause some worry. The finest minds have differed about political philosophy, and the very foundations of our culture were laid by Greek thinkers whose pursuit of political wisdom has never been equalled. Why should Christians start praying for the reconciliation of differences which may well express some of the best human instincts? It is, presumably, because they suppose the differences of view, and the attrition of philosophies, can be accommodated by discussion. Yet the baneful record of human society suggests that they very rarely are. The twentieth century saw the first mass education, the first large-scale democratic practice, and the first popular dissemination of knowledge: the result was the most horrific warfare, and unparalleled acts of sheer human nastiness. When Christians pray for peace they should not be, in effect, trying to promote an agenda for compromise. They should recognize that serious differences of view are actually the raw material of human advance, which promote ideological maturity. Humans are thinking creatures, not animals to be mollified. Authentic peace, God's peace, is a condition of the heart. It is unlikely, alas, in view of the human record, that it will ever receive institutional embodiment.

Fifty Nine

Loyalty to truth

೮つಲಿ

Fifty years ago it was a fringe of 'Modernist' theologians, and a handful of eccentric bishops, who interpreted the central miraculous characteristics of the life of Christ – the divinity of Christ and his Resurrection – as symbolical rather than actual. There has been an extraordinary change. Today it is the upholders of belief in the corporeal Resurrection who are regarded as controversial, and many leaders of Anglican opinion are increasingly hesitant to express the nature of Christ's divinity in plain language. There is, in every age, a disposition to reinterpret the past according to the orthodoxies and fashions of ideas of the present; what now seems to be happening is that Christian thinkers and some leaders – including many priests in the parishes – are simply incapable of resisting the prevalent secular Humanism, and are evidently prepared to consider it intellectually mature to ditch the miraculous interpretation of the nature of Christ in order to recognize, as they suppose, his supreme human and ethicist qualities. The doctrine of the Resurrection is the most crucial test of orthodoxy in Christianity precisely because the tradition of believers, which for two thousand years has created the Christ of our understanding by witnessing to what the first disciples of the Saviour believed, has been united to a literal and physical interpretation. Many Anglicans now suppose that Christ's risen presence among his followers was not corporeal, but that somehow it was his love and his care for humanity which returned to their senses, and became his personality, in a spiritualized sense.

There are two principal reasons why this revision of received teaching is inherently unlikely to be true. Both are historical.

117

First, the modern adherent to the Faith is now being asked to imagine that the earliest followers of Jesus existed in a religious culture which was liable to understand 'resurrection' symbolically. They lived, it is true, at a time when truth was often expressed in elaborate and sustained allegories – but that is not the same as symbolism. Nor, it must be emphasized, was knowledge about resurrection obscure. The Greek and Egyptian cults of the time, and some of those from the Euphrates, were full of resurrection myths, in which dead divinities rose from their graves: in none of them was the central event regarded as symbolical. Osiris no less than Christ was regarded as having a corporeal resurrection. From the very beginning those who acclaimed the Risen Lord believed that it was the man they had known and loved, and not some memory of him, however fragrant, who appeared to them in the garden of burial, in the upper room, on the road to Emmaus, by the lake shore, and at the Ascension. The second reason why the doctrine of the Resurrection is to be taken historically is that the tradition of believers requires it. If the succession of Christian understanding, for which we are indebted for *all* our knowledge of Christianity, has wrongly interpreted the Resurrection as a physical event for two thousand years, about what else is its witness to be judged unreliable? The truth is that Christ entrusted his message, and the knowledge of his life, to a body of believers – the Church – and it is impossible to separate Christian truth from the tradition they have transmitted. And why do so anyway? Are the treasures of eternity to be thrown away because an increasing number of modern Anglicans are incapable of recognizing their value?

Sixty

A shared identity

⁍⁌

It will be regrettable if Christians in this country re-identify themselves as belonging to what are now commonly being called 'Faith Communities'. This designation has become current for what are doubtless laudable reasons: a desire to recognize the integrity of the non-Christian religions represented in the nation's composition, and a practical acceptance that this is a plural society. But Christians are members not of a 'Faith Community' but of a Church. To the extent that the Church of Christ is a 'community' at all it is an eternal one, most of whose members are in the celestial society. Those believers who at present exist in the world are only, by definition, a 'community' in a highly qualified sense, despite the great weight of opinion within the present leadership which would categorize the Christian religion in social rather than doctrinal terms – as essentially a matter of caring for humanity rather than of right belief about the nature of God. The call of Christ is for individual repentance; it is the corruption intrinsic to each person which is addressed in the Gospels, and the forgiveness which is the superlative gift of the Christian religion is given to each person and not to collectives. Of course the Church is a *society*, and the first members were gathered and sent out by Jesus himself with the clear intention that they would, at the local level, establish his presence and his message within people living in actual communities. To be effective evangelistically, and to practise religious virtue both among themselves and towards those among whom they were sent, Christians constituted distinct social association. But the Church as such is the body of Christ in the world – his very presence, his truth conveyed in the loyalty to his teaching of those who submit to his supreme authority. The Church is thus primarily and overwhelmingly a body dedicated to teaching truth. And so it is exclusive in the sense that its truth is precise and demanding, and inclusive in the sense that anyone can be received. Indeed, the Church is, according to Christ himself, for sinners: he came for the lost, and the first to be admitted to Paradise was the thief who was crucified with him.

To classify the body of the Lord as one among a number of 'Faith Communities' may be satisfactory enough for external observers; for Christians themselves, however, it is not an accurate description. In real terms, what does it amount to? The average parish congregation meets once a week for worship; it has a fringe of enthusiasts who gather for specialist activities and to foster a sense of social camaraderie. Is this what is meant by 'community'? They share very few values, allowing themselves to derive most of their beliefs – seemingly even their religious ones – on an individualistic basis. Their lives are passed in separated social units, and in England the Church membership discloses strong social class characteristics. Is this the lower bourgeoisie at prayer? To accept the description of 'Faith Community' is to adopt a sectarian self-identity, and the Church of England, which is still evidently willing to persist as an Established Church, must surely find this yet another contradiction to add to its rather full hand of mutually conflicting attributes.

Sixty One

Illusions about death

ଽଠୡଷ

The commemoration of All Souls yesterday had more extensive
resonances than once could have been anticipated. A few
decades ago it would have been marked, in this country, within
the Catholic Church, and by some in the Anglo-Catholic congregations of the Church of England. But as a popular cultic
event the ritualized commemoration of the departed had
dropped out of public consciousness at the Reformation, and
even the children's celebration of Hallowe'en was a pretty
muted affair. That has all changed, and the marking of the
day of the departed has been secularized. Under, largely, the
irresistible allure of American commercial agencies, it has
recently become a major attraction: the dead are remembered
in a festival of the macabre, shop-window displays exhibit
grinning skulls, surprised infants are presented with sweets
fashioned to resemble ghosts. Despite appearances this is not a
ghoulish enterprise – it's all innocent generation of capitalist
profit, without apparent theological or religious significance.

Or is it? The modern revival of popular interest in the
supposedly paranormal has prompted a quite unexpected
regeneration of old-fashioned superstition. It is religion
replaced by magic. Of course, the votaries of all the films and
books about the supernatural would assert that they don't really
believe in it. They are part, nevertheless, of the creation of a
popular culture which, like science fiction, has a way of being
made into a sort of reality – in that it becomes the cultural
reference within which people make choices about other ideas,
and ones which are truly important. Thus expectations about
religion today tend to include the satisfaction of the kinds of

imagined experiences conveyed in works about the super-natural which were originally written solely for entertainment. The public now has a taste for religion of emotional gratifica-tion; to be acceptable, that is to say, the Church has to purvey an understanding of Christianity which has a high entertainment level – it has to make an immediate appeal to the senses. But the call of Jesus was to the inherent propensity to evil in each person; he offered forgiveness, not for what our emotions tell us is wrong about ourselves, but for that which is actually and objectively wrong. People today look to religion to give them 'uplift' or personal significance; the religion of Jesus, however, is about conviction of sin.

The commemoration of the departed, in its new secularized acceptance, has another hazardous dimension. It encourages the modern resurgence of belief in individual communication with the dead. This remains, perhaps, a fringe belief still: yet there are indications, again with evidences to be drawn from popular entertainment, that the numbers are growing of those who are disposed to imagine themselves able in some way to establish a contact with the dead. In Christian belief, it must be emphasized, however, the departed lose the kind of identities they had in life, and are changed. How easily we persist in contemplating heaven as a painless version of the earth.

Sixty Two

Loving the unlovely

ജ‌ൽ

It is usually reasonably easy to love those who are possessed of attractive qualities: Christianity demands love of those who are vile. There was probably no time in Christian history when this was more difficult, since the moral culture of Western societies today projects an optimistic view of human nature which is utterly unlike the way most people actually are. Yet the unfavourable contrast does not appear to upset the basic belief, now so widespread, that humanity is essentially good, and that individual men and women are so worthwhile that they deserve immortality. The last point is meant seriously. Christians have always followed the words of Christ himself in teaching that at the end of the world there is judgement, and that, like the sheep and the goats, the people of the world will be divided between the virtuous, or those aspiring with all their strengths to virtue, and the corrupt. Today, however, there is a strong tide flowing against discrimination of any kind when it comes to human worth; almost everyone who bothers to think about it, including probably a majority of Christian believers, suppose that *everyone* merits eternal life. A few rotten apples are, it is true, left in the barrel: paedophiles and mass murderers – the demons singled out by the press – racists and perhaps drug-dealers, have no place in the secular Kingdom of the righteous. But in general modern people are universalists, and the elevated estimate human nature now obtains will not allow for any statistically significant numbers to be destined for extinction. When everyone is thought to be so lovely, how is it that real people, the people of everyday encounter, can be so awful? The contrast is left tantalizingly unrecognized. Christians, as a matter of religious belief, see humanity as deeply flawed; for them love of the dreadful becomes a real discipline, a means of achieving spiritual growth in the moral attrition of familiar experience. For the Humanists, on the other hand, for whom men and women are doctrinally essentially good, the frequent confrontation with the plain evidence of the wrongness of their convictions appears undisturbing. So the awful characteristics of others become attributed to the chances of social conditioning. Love of neighbour, a popular concept in a secularized sense, can be interpreted within a culture of welfare entitlements and other provisions of the state – which can be made at second remove and do not require personal involvement. There also exists, to be frank, a large category of pathological moralists, who would have been officials of the Church in the ages of faith and are today drawn either professionally or privately to interfering in the lives of others.

Christianity, in contrast, is about the love of neighbour. And love hurts, it involves real sacrifice, it goes against the grain of our natures in all but the most favoured circumstances, it exists indiscriminately in relation to the good and the bad, and it makes us like Christ. It was for sinners that Jesus came into the world, and for them – for all of us – that he died. Christianity is the religion of the flawed and the corrupted, and that describes the whole race. The intrinsic pessimism about human nature in the Christian view of things is more than compensated by a supreme optimism about the great love of God. The sign of its presence is when people love one another, not because they are nice but because they share the universality of sin.

Sixty Three

The God who may be known

ಏಂಡ

Prayer is the means whereby the individual believer, and the Church corporately, maintains a relationship with God. It is not a kind of adjunct or optional dimension to the Christian life: it is absolutely essential. Prayer, furthermore, cannot by its nature be abstract – God, to be addressed with any real meaning, has to be known personally. In the Christian doctrine of the Trinity he is represented as *persons*, and so may be conceived in the only images available to the people of the world. Our knowledge of the Divine derives from our conditioning by the circumstances of life on earth; these are conveyed to us in language and symbols and in the ordered assembly of sequences of understanding we call culture. In the Judaic-Christian spiritual culture God is understood to have revealed his nature and his purposes – or, at least, enough of his nature and purposes for us to enter a relationship with him – and to have established laws which enable men and women to obey his will. In the Christian revelation, God himself came into the world. This great act of self-giving not only provided for our redemption, but it also confirmed that God can be known about, in Christ, as a *person*. If you would know God, then know Jesus.

This is all primary Christianity. Yet it needs to be spelled out afresh in our age since the secularization of the concept of 'spirituality' – so that it is now conventionally taken to refer to merely human accomplishments which appear to elevate emotional sensation – leads many to imagine that 'prayer' can somehow be addressed, as a species of therapy, to some abstract spirit of goodness. It is a concept found frequently in the cults of the ancient world, and constitutes, to put it bluntly, a kind of pagan revivalism. To the modern understanding 'God' can be encountered in 'meditative' contemplation of art and music and poetry, and so forth: all artefacts of humanity which may indeed honour attributes of the Creator but which, more commonly, reflect merely the emotional conditioning of earthly experience. In the Christian religion worship is adorned with the best the world can offer. That is *all* that happens, however. Adornment is an accident of a process in which God is addressed directly as a Person by persons. He is not an aesthetic impulse or an abstract representation of worldly perceptions of beauty. Nor is he a moral icon – a super version of human attempts to control social exchange by regulatory apparatus. God *is*: his being is known to men and women in ways established by him, in distinct traditions of spiritual interpretation. These have to be learned: traditions of understanding, whether they refer to the manner of weaving a cloth or perceiving the nature of the Divine, are not self-explanatory. The appropriate skills and the right vocabulary have to be adopted. In the ancient world religious specialities were recognized as *mysteries* – their truths, that is to say, were revealed to initiates only after extensive and lengthy preparation. How enormously this contrasts with the modern expectation that the spiritual truths revealed to the ancients only after years of study will be available to the understanding of today at the press of a computer keyboard or the viewing of a television documentary.

Sixty Four

Religionless religion

෫0Ꮕ෩

The recent calls for more Church secondary schools, made by prominent figures within the Church of England and with the apparent support of the government, are not to be taken as serious attempts at the evangelization of society. Far from it. From statements and explanations of policy made by the same leaders it is quite clear that the Christian virtues to be conveyed in the proposed schools – as, presumably, in the existing ones – are social rather than doctrinal. Ever since the practical adoption of a report of 1970, produced by a Church commission under the chairmanship of the then Bishop of Durham, it has been the conventional wisdom of Anglicanism that the children in Church schools, no less than those in state schools, should not be 'indoctrinated' with Christianity but should be presented with a wide range of knowledge about all the major religions so that they may, in due time, make up their own minds. Agreed local syllabuses, and the requirements of half-implemented educational legislation, accord well with this policy. The children in Church schools, therefore, are in general not *instructed* in Christianity; they receive an *education* in religion sufficiently broad to enable them to respect the tenets of the main available brands. Parents favour Church schools because they have a reputation for encouraging moral decency: there seems little indication that they, any more than the bishops, are interested in the conveyance of doctrinal truths. The exponents of the proposed new Church schools emphasize that what will make them distinctive is not evangelization – or even the association of the acquisition of secular knowledge with religious teaching – but the 'embodiment' of applied

'Christian' attitudes of 'caring'. It is plain that once again it is the agreed common enthusiasm for human values which is going to be re-interpreted as basic Christianity. The schools are to have a Christian 'atmosphere', to propagate a Christian 'ethos'. And that seems to be understood without reference to the actual instruction of the young in Christian doctrine. The Church schools established by the Church of England in the nineteenth century were plainly intended to provide for the future of Christianity; they were a means of instructing children in the doctrines of the religion. Even that purpose is now being reinterpreted: modern educationalists now insist that the Church schools were originally intended as a sort of social service – to provide education rather than religion. Historical revisionism, as always, is born of modern social doctrine.

The truth is that people today, both inside and outside the Church, are impatient with the concept of Christianity as a structure of precise doctrine. What they seek is religion as personal therapy, as aesthetic sensation, as emotional uplift, as a celebration of warm human qualities and a parade of esteemed human virtues. The liberal Anglicans who set the terms of reference within which the Church of England's educational institutions have their being appear to espouse an understanding of the nature of religion which is scarcely distinguishable from the conventional check list. This is religion as a catalogue of public issues, of campaigns for humanity, the resort of the politically correct, the elevation of the secular. Christianity, however, begins with regret for human sin.

Sixty Five

On dying well

𝕾𝖔𝖈𝖘

It is a duty of all Christians to help others prepare for death. For the Christian, after all, the most important thing in life is leaving it: the final attainment of blessedness is the heavenly consequence for those who have tried to accept Christ's calling and to have commended themselves to the mercy of God. Nothing so requires the witness of other Christian souls and their prayers. Every Christian death is attended by the unseen presence of the celestial society, and that is sufficient in itself to consecrate the departure from the earth of those whom the Lord beckons into the greater light of eternity. Then the eternal life gathered by the aspirant Christian during the earthly pilgrimage is translated to Paradise and receives an unknowable fulfilment. But each soul also needs, where that is possible, the assistance and the courage of others, to be present at the time of death, to reassure in the event of gathering doubt – a common enough occurrence – to urge acts of contrition, to join in prayers of commendation. In traditional society 'a good death' was a public event; family, friends, the priest, and close associates would be present to assist the dying person in the great last agony.

Today, in horrific contrast – the more horrific for not being recognized as such – death usually takes place in the relative anonymity of a hospital bed; the departing soul incapable through the administration of hallucinogenic pain-killing medication of a considered response to the awful solemnity of the occasion; and the gathering crowd of witnesses are not the attentive friends but the bureaucrats of the hospital anxious to see that documentation and the administration of the death are regularized according to the official procedures. The medical staffs are, of course, trained to call a priest if the circumstances will allow; it is in the nature of things, however, that medically controlled deaths do not often take place in circumstances which favour it. Most Christian souls now depart from the world without the immediate prayers of the living and without the chance of final confession of sin. The relatives often conspire, beforehand, to keep from the dying the gravity of the clinical condition. They offer, indeed, all kinds of quite false assurances about the possibility of survival. The clergy are not blameless either, promising eternal blessedness to the dying without taking the necessary technical measures – such as the eliciting of confession – which actually assists it. There is also not wanting a suspicion that nursing staffs acquiesce in all this: a ward of dying people who are encouraged to imagine they have a prospect of survival is easier to manipulate than one in which the stark truth is recognized.

Christians need to die with realism, and always to be conscious that beyond the grave lies a fate which for so very many may prove truly terrible. When Jesus spoke of the coming judgement he was not speaking in images or using the vocabulary of symbolism. Christians know that they are called to account, and that life itself is not at the disposal of their personal desires, but is the preparation for an eternal existence which God wills.

Sixty Six

True exultation

ೞಞ

Amidst all the talk about a babe in a manger, and the ritual condemnation of the supposedly excessive commercialization, and the pieties about remembering the unfortunates excluded from the festive goings-on, it is easy for Christians to forget that what they are celebrating at Christmas is the birth of a King. It was a King who was laid in a manager by his blessed mother: the great paradox of the Christian religion is that the Creator of all things, the Lord of the earth, came into his own not in state and majesty, but in the humblest of circumstances. Yet the attributes of Kingship were always present. The child, the record carefully points out, was a descendant of the royal line of David; it was in pursuit of a King that the wise men, in symbolical representation, made their quest; and it was through fear of a rival for his actual throne that Herod sought to eliminate potential aspirants, however young. It is the sovereignty of Jesus which is now so often neglected, despite the clear insistence on it in the biblical accounts of the birth of Christ. Jesus is Lord. And that applies to the details in the individual lives of believers. The Christmas story is not to be received, as it now so often is, as a mawkish celebration of what are, in the end, merely human sentiments – but as the occasion to surrender to a sovereign. This should not be a kitsch carnival of paraded humanitarian intentions, or, worse, lauded sentimentality about wonder in the starry-eyed delight of children, as they rip open cascading packages beneath the tree on Xmas morning. This is in reality the season when Christians should re-submit themselves to the commands of God, and to remember that Jesus came into the world, and suffered death, because of *our* sins. The celebration is of the gift of redemption; the joy derives from voluntary integration with the everlasting society of those who are subjects of Christ.

In recent years the Christmas festival has been increasingly secularized in America, and there are signs, already, that the trend will reproduce itself here. It is getting difficult in America to buy greetings cards with the words 'Happy Christmas' (or even 'Merry Xmas'): the politically correct versions – now already the staple – declare 'Happy Holiday Season'. Television advertising, comparably, peddles goods on the basis of a secular understanding of the celebration. There are protests about placing Christmas trees, or other symbols which are associated with the Christian festival, in or near public buildings. Perhaps, if the concept of a society of plural values is taken seriously, this is a logical consequence. But it is sad, nonetheless, to witness the deconsecration of public life. So let Christians, at any rate among themselves, and at any rate in Britain, continue to mark the birth of their sovereign Lord and King with undisguised fervour. And let their rejoicing resonate with authentic religious sentiment. Christian truth receives its embodiment in the world where men and women receive Christ into their lives – and make him the sovereign of their being. Life on earth was not intended to become the texture of gentle inconsequence we so often make it: God calls us to a life which, through submission to his will, achieves a quality which can rightly be identified as eternal.

Sixty Seven

Of religious truth

ℬℭ

It has now become fashionable for all those who regard themselves as intellectually enlightened to consider all religions as
basically the same – among those, that is to say, who are prepared to judge religion worth bothering with at all. The idea is
that God – or 'the spiritual', as Humanists are given to describe
the finer instincts of mankind – can be known about in all kinds
of ways, and that the main religious traditions of the world with
their cultural phenomena are apparently happy to proceed
further, and to envisage a species of synthesized religion in
which adherents of the diverse faiths come together in the
basics that are imagined to unite them. These common features
or core beliefs actually become too generalized, in their understanding of God, to be capable of expression in any meaningful
act of worship, or else in reality amount to the worship of characteristics of humanity itself – its capacity to experience a sense
of the beautiful, for example, or the good. This second tendency
in fact renders religious belief as a brand of ethicism, and turns
out to be a sanctimonious way for the high-minded to describe
ordinary moral seriousness. This Neo-Deism, or however generalized religion is to be described, is now being propagated by
Western governments and welfare agencies of governments,
by schoolteachers, by television journalists, and – no surprise
here – by liberal clergymen. Their line is that emphasis on the
doctrines of each religion cultivates social division, and in effect
wrecks the dream of ethnic parity (since the major world
religions as represented in a plural society like Britain's can
be identified in race categories). There are already the first
rumblings of political objection to state subsidy of Church

schools on precisely these grounds. Interestingly, it is liberals in the former Christian cultures of the West who are the exponents of universal latitudinarianism, together with a tiny fringe of Westernized leaders of Islam. Are they positing a claim to have achieved a superior insight into the nature of religion than the exponents of the non-Christian religions, whose ideals and practices remain exclusivist? In the decaying and declining leadership of the Western Christian Churches religious truth is being understood in an increasingly less precise manner; it is the ethical teachings of Christianity, rather than its former claims about the nature of God, which are currently esteemed. It is just a matter of time until inter-faith worship becomes widely promoted as quintessentially Christian.

Christians, however, have always believed that Christ died for the redemption of humanity, and that the forgiveness he holds out may only be received after repentance and the individual confession of the sovereignty of God. This is a very precise demand, and it requires personal submission to a precise Person, to Jesus. That involves doctrine: the establishment of the religious pedigree of Christ, of his relationship to the other Persons of the Trinity, of the authority of his continuing divine mission in the Church – his body in the world. These are not generalities, or ideals which are compatible with rival under-standings about God's dealings with his creatures. Charity calls for sympathy and ecclesiastical courtesy between peoples of different faiths; but all religions are *not* the same. The man who does not enter the sheepfold by the gate, but climbs in by some other way, is a thief and a robber. Those are the words of Christ.

Sixty Eight

The promise of truth

೫಄ಬ

Christianity is what Christians say it is. They are guided, of course, by Scripture and by the interpretations and practices of their predecessors in the faith. Yet those are not, in themselves, stable guidelines or authorities. Scripture itself was compiled out of a large number of alternative sacred texts, by the Church. The process was not completed until two centuries after the death of Christ. And as for tradition, the tradition of the believers through two thousand years, that, too, has shown too many evidences of dissension and controversy, and actual schism in the general body, to be unambiguously reliable as a source of authority. Or has it? Whitsun is an assurance that the tradition of believers is indeed reliable, but the matter needs careful, and technical, interpretation.

There are plenty of evidences in the New Testament itself of arguments among the first Christians about how they were to receive, and then to transmit, their saving faith in Christ. The culture in which they operated was overwhelmingly Greek: even educated Jews were deeply Hellenized, as was, to some extent, their understanding of their own religion. Yet the first Christians had to cope with a situation in which distinctively Jewish religious ideas and practices had to be adapted to the modules of interpretation available to non-Jews. In addition the whole was organized by a Roman political system which was tolerant of local religions, where they remained local, but was suspicious of those who carried their zeal for conversions into parts of the Empire where a disruption of the peace was a probable consequence. Since the Romans, too, were in religious and cultural terms deeply Hellenized there was an available single world of reference which, to some extent, assisted the translation of ideas across boundaries. Into this complicated situation came God himself: Jesus lived a real life at the very congruence of religious mixture. How do we know, in view of all the consequent disputes among Christians themselves, that what we have received from them – and after two thousand years of revisionism – is an authentic version of the truth of Christ?

The answer is celebrated at Whitsun: God's gift of himself in the Person of the Holy Spirit. Christ's body in the world is the Church: the company of the believers whom he instructed and sent out in his name to evangelize the countryside and towns of Galilee and Judea, and for whom he appointed twelve leaders. That body was, and still is, quite a small number of people, as Jesus himself had indicated: many are called, he said, but few are chosen; many, he said again, will call on my name but will not be authentic followers. The body of the Lord, the Church, has developed and reinterpreted the truths conveyed by Jesus in ways compatible with the dialectical shifts in the human cultures through which the Church has travelled over the centuries, and it is still here today, witnessing, as ever, to the sovereignty and mercy of God. That the believers' understanding of Christianity is truly what God wills it to be is guaranteed by the Holy Spirit, as, again, Jesus promised explicitly. Each person may hear his word in his own tongue, but the message is the same. The fire of the Spirit may illuminate different dimensions from different angles in different places: but it is the same Lord who is in all. Whitsun is a time for rejoicing and consolation. For the God we love is God indeed.

Sixty Nine

———

The Jubilee

ಲಂಜ

A leading advantage of the existence of the monarchy in the present circumstances of the United Kingdom is that it reminds politicians that they are *not* the State. Modern political processes unavoidably encourage short-term thinking in public figures: their calculations are set upon the accommodation of public opinion, elections have to be won, media commentary has to be included in estimates of the effect of actions, and the entire practice of liberal democracy, in short, stimulates a populist approach to serious issues which politicians deny yet cultivate with careful strategies. Perhaps there is a deception behind all this – or, to express it more favourably to the politicians, perhaps some of their notions of what they are engaged in are illusory. Public life today is all about the manipulation of opinion, the management of information, the representation of policy and events in a manner which coincides with popular prejudice. But all the time, behind the scenes in the drama of democratic processes, elites are actually setting up the terms of reference within which public life is conducted. Their schemes, however, rarely look further than the next election, and their much-displayed moral concern generally disguises political self-interest. Those who describe the operations of present politics as they actually are usually get accused of cynicism; theirs, as it happens, is simple realism. In the modern world, so it seems, presentation is everything, and principled governance is a low priority.

Hereditary monarchy, in contrast, offers an example of selfless service which achieves a measure of disinterest now almost unknown in the political realm. The hereditary element achieves detachment from the squalid canvassing of half-truths which currently describes the process by which political choice is made at times of transition; it guarantees that the choice of Head of State, the symbol of the nation's self-identity, is detached from the transient passions which distort all other political management in the life of the country. It is precisely the symbolical aspect of monarchy in a Constitution which has come, by pragmatic adjustment, to operate democratically, that is to be judged of great value. A nation needs a focus of its legitimacy as a sovereign unit, an organic link with its past, and, in times of extremely rapid change like the present, a sure transmission of its idea of itself to the future. Monarchy today also requires – and this is in some contrast with the past – that the person of the monarch shall be virtuous. And that is much more difficult to arrange. Indeed the veneration of celebrity, which is so prominent a feature of modern popular opinion, actually operates very disadvantageously in reverse – the famous who fall from grace, whose less than worthy habits or conduct are disclosed to a public anxious to believe the worst of anybody, are shown little mercy. Lesser members of the Royal Family have found this to their cost. The person of the sovereign, however, fulfils a symbolical role, and hereditary monarchy still works extremely well even in modern conditions. Now the sovereign is unfortunate enough to have to devote her life to the fearful task of being a symbol of something – national identity – which is difficult to define. Church and state can give thanks at this time for a sovereign who is religious and dutiful, the very image of the unchanging and untarnished higher ideal which the nation's history and culture have sought to promote.

Enduring all things

ഋൟൟ

People in society today seem unable, or disinclined, to put up with the misfortunes which always afflicted humanity. Some of these misfortunes, it is true, can be avoided by a rearrangement of the manner in which society operates; they can be cured by reform. But the overwhelming majority cannot. There are things like unhappy marriage, or ungrateful children, or frustrated ambition, or unsuitable work, or incurable disease, or loneliness and the dreadful effects of old age in limiting personal choice and mobility. This last condition, in fact, may demonstrate how difficult it sometimes is to distinguish between afflictions over which there is virtually no human control and those which are the consequence of avoidable choices. The same medical advances which have enabled us to remove some types of physical pain have also, combined with environmental improvements, produced a lengthening of the average lifespan. People seem very eager that this should be the case. But there is, for very many now, no clear religious or philosophical goals which are considered the purpose of life – let alone an extended one – and the additional years would seem to contribute little either to human wisdom or to personal development. They are spent, indeed, in conditions of growing bodily discomfort and emotional loneliness. Without an identifiable purpose life in decrepitude can be a burden which few would rationally choose but very many as a matter of record are seemingly glad to endure. Sometimes, of course, their condition is involuntary – forced upon them by well-meaning relatives who urge every medical means of keeping loved ones alive upon a medical profession which is terrified of being subject to formal scrutiny should some procedure or other remain unused. It is a very difficult area. 'Ethical considerations', as defined and practised, are not much help, since they are evidently devised by committees whose ethical criteria appear to be supplied by an inclination to do whatever alleviates human bodily suffering rather than by reference to any objective or traditional corpus of philosophical or religious thought.

All that apart – and it is an area which needs proper scrutiny – the fact that suffering is in so many cases caused by things which are insoluble remains inexplicit in the judgement of most people. We rush to blame others, or social structures, or government, for ills which have always visited men and women since social consciousness began. The Christian religion actually has much to say about this, and it teaches acceptance of personal misfortune, rather than blaming others, and the conversion of affliction into the raw material of spiritual formation. Jesus told his followers to love their enemies, to walk the other mile, to forgive the brother who sins against them, and to endure the sufferings of the present life for his sake. The Christian life meant taking up the Cross, not fuming with outrage because your children do not behave as they might. In small things and in large the exhortations and example of Christ direct his followers to suffer for his sake, and to recognize that for thinking creatures much in life will illustrate the disagreeable mismatch between what we can imagine as the ideal and what human circumstances actually deliver. 'Take no thought', Jesus said to those who might be inclined to seek bodily comfort: we are called to higher things than that.

೮ƆCೆ

Seventy One

A *danse macabre*

ಐⱭᏟᏰ

There is a category of dramatic events which seems to visit the emotional condition of people in modern society and excite them to public spasms of grief. Thus the scenes which accompanied the Hillsborough disaster, the death of Diana, the Eleventh of September. Then people deposited heaps of flowers and, to the scarcely disguised delight of the clergy, even attended church services. These same clergy also rushed to identify each infusion of worshippers as a sign that the people were residually religious, and just needed some particularly searing happening to trawl their inherent spirituality to the surface. But these outpourings of public grief cannot really indicate any such thing. They are, for a start, rather unhealthy happenings: the emotional springs of action in the individuals affected would not appear to have been fed by the memory of collected religious teaching but by histrionics. The afflicted were engaging in an emotional release which was inward-looking, essentially an exercise in introspective indulgence of the self-importance of personal response. People – or rather, women, for women are better at unconscious grief therapy than men are – went to church because the social culture does not at present provide alternative venues for the public demonstration of vicarious grief. This disagreeable but probably true observation does not exclude the simultaneous existence of authentic personal regret at the death of others. Yet people are dying all the time, and it is only with the demise of celebrities, or where mass extinctions occur in circumstances of particular horror (as in a rail or an air disaster), that individuals allow themselves extremes of public grief. It is their own sense of shock which is then celebrated, rather than real knowledge of the dead or the circumstances of death. There is also grief by association. A well-known person who once seemed to characterize a generation, or a decade, or a moment of popular culture, passes from the world and people are bathed in nostalgic waters of sad yet somehow satisfying remembrance. And off they go to church, recalling another feature of a world they have lost. But it does not last. In a couple of weeks the churches are empty again, and the vicars are ruefully counting the days till the next infusion of seeming support. It is a hard view; it is also a fallen humanity, and emotional self-indulgence, like indulgence of every sort, is a feature of the times.

Christian belief does not rest on emotional satisfaction but on obedience to the revealed will of God. Acceptance of reality means recognizing that the Creation was set up by God for his purposes and not for ours. Humans share with all living things a precarious and short life on the surface of this unstable planet, and, in relationship to its Creator, they have no rights and no reasonable expectation to release from pain and suffering. God sends us occasions of joy; we debase them by demanding them as standard issue. Our response to tragedy should not be inspired by what it does to our emotional condition but in how it can help us to accept the divine purpose. Hence authentic stoicism, and not sensationalism, will help us to advance in spiritual wisdom, and to let the dead bury their dead.

Seventy Two

———

Along the way

 🙰🙰

It is the time of year, sometimes the only time in the year, when people travel; it is the time for holidays. Most of this travel, therefore, is undertaken for pleasure – in contrast to the journeys made by most of our predecessors. In truly nomadic societies of the ancient world movement was linked to actual survival, and life itself became a literal progression through the world, an unending homelessness by those for whom the journey was all they experienced of social reality. Imagine, therefore, the gratitude of the people of Israel when they found, and conquered, land for themselves – and for ever afterwards made their expression of gratitude to God the basis of their religious understanding. For many people in the past the journey they entered upon was the pilgrimage: an odyssey of the soul to offer thanks in a different way – by prayer at a shrine. Modern writers, largely on the evidence of Chaucer's pilgrims, have tended to represent all pilgrimage as a disguised form of vacation, and have thus anachronistically adhered their own lack of serious spiritual purpose to the searing expectations of their medieval and earlier predecessors. In the Greek world pilgrims journeyed in order to consult an oracle about choice of proposed action; both then and at most other times people have travelled to healing sanctuaries, seeking relief from affliction through the mercy of the divine presence in a holy well or a school of sacred cultic observances. As we journey today, to Miami, let us say, or to Genoa, our intentions may be very different, but we, too, still experience something of the detachment from familiar surroundings, and the hope of fresh insights, which those people of the past looked for in their wanderings. Even we, for all the materialism of our circum-stances, and the removal of most (but not quite all) sense of personal hazard from the business of locomotion, can still sense that we are in transition in more than a merely bodily fashion.

The image of life as a journey has always been used in the religious life, and this continues to attract modern exponents of Christianity. Yet the sense in which individual lives are forever in transit has changed radically. Our predecessors used the idea to show how the soul, having been claimed by Christ through initiation into his Faith, faces all kinds of dangers on its course through the world, how it is tested by each one, and is educated in spiritual formation as a consequence, arriving eventually at a triumphant entry into Paradise. Some modern users of the image – and it is becoming the conventional use among Christians today – conceive the journey of life to be itself a *discovery* of faith: that the experiences of the world, collectively, provide the content of spiritual understanding. This second usage reflects the modern disposition for people, regarding themselves as emancipated from religious authority, to con-struct a menu of religious ideas by eclectic association, and to consider the resulting and very personal mix to be 'Christianity'. Many of the clergy today encourage them in such endeavours, seeing the procedure as evidence of mature understanding. But Jesus warned his followers that many would come in his name with false ideas. The authentic Christian journey is a pilgrimage through the world of the whole People of God together, confessing the same truths and enduring all things. And led by the great shepherd of their souls.

Seventy Three

The lover of souls

The God worshipped by Christians is both universal and particular. He is, that is to say, evenly present throughout his Creation and yet may be known about because he has chosen to reveal himself. Christ comes to us as God in the form of – and truly – humanity: in the vocabulary and images which men and women had contrived to socialize themselves he spoke of the divine purposes and called for the obedience of individual lives to the divine will. Though familiarity has robbed this astonishing act of mercy of its capacity to enthral us it remains, still, the essential Christian statement – God is concerned with his creatures and makes himself known to them. Revelation, however, is precise. Jesus, when in the world, described very exactly how the corrupted condition of humanity, and its seemingly perpetual exchange of authentic spiritual priorities for expendable simulations, requires amendment of personal beliefs and conduct. And herein is the great love of God. It is not, as modern enquirers after truth sometimes imagine, that he resides in whatever moves the individual senses, but that he offers precise knowledge about the terms of salvation to those who very definitely do not deserve them.

In Christ's words, furthermore, lay *instruction* in the ways of God. People suppose themselves somehow qualified to construct religious ideas for themselves, selecting images and propositions which accommodate their understanding of beauty or personal significance – or a generalized sense of human value, rendered in sentimentalized cultures of over-optimistic assessments of human nature. The Greeks knew that you can only properly derive a knowledge of universal laws by observation of particular embodiments of them. Modern people, on the contrary, appear to operate upon the contention that the universal lies within themselves, and that it is their emotional needs which religion exists to clothe with meaning and spiritual splendour. Jesus declared bluntly that men and women were sinners unqualified to deliver their own redemption. Yet the modern pursuit of self-derived religion is exactly that: an attempt to redeem the person without reference to the external existence of divine commands. Perhaps never before in the history and prehistory of the race were humans less qualified to construct religious understanding for themselves. Now they do it with an assertive abandon. They do it, additionally, by reducing religion to generalities. All religions are fundamentally the same, they suppose; the differences indicate merely cultural and geographical diversities. But a God who is imagined to disclose himself in such a generalized manner is a God without a knowable nature. Love requires a content, and content means exact revelation, and revelation came with the teaching of Jesus – who loved the fallen creatures of the world so much that he died for them.

Seventy Four

Getting the human perspective right

℘℆

The surface of the planet is coated with life; we are a part of it, integrated with the teeming abundance and chaotic superfluity which since the beginning has evolved and developed for purposes which are not self-evident. The capacity of humanity for reason and reflection has given us, it is true, a series of insights into the mechanics of the Creation – and also a virtually unquestioned assertiveness about the claims of our species to sovereign disposal of worldly resources. Looked at in the order of nature, men and women have only the meaning attached by themselves to their own significance; the most successful life-form to date, the most given to critical evaluation of their own condition, and the most selfish. With the intellectual possibility of contriving a serene social order the reality is a human record of horrific indulgence in every kind of vile crime against our coexisters. In earlier stages of human self-consciousness – in, let us say, the societies of Greece or Rome – enormous advances were made in appreciation of the subtleties of ideas and the categorization of social reality. Men and women were then recognized for what they are: flawed creatures, achieving a frail moral purchase upon a living order in which they were no more than transients. Today, despite our great advances in understanding and in manipulating the mechanics of Creation, men and women have fallen into the most dreadful spiritual barbarism. The first sign of this is their unreasonable claim to exemption from their mere humanity. They seek the immunity of immortals from the ordinary processes of mutual absorption and death which describe the nature of all life on earth. Having used the reason given to them by God to discover so much about the means by which he ordered his Creation to operate they now demand personal exclusion from the inevitable consequences of personal decay.

Nearly all of the problems of humans today derive from their simple lack of realism. Christians, however, know that the only value possessed by human life is what God ordains; they know that it is his will which has, for the time being, admitted them to a communion with the infinite. Whatever gives them a superiority over the rest of the living mass is solely a gift from God, and is held, furthermore, on terms which he himself has revealed – in the tradition of religious belief given by God in the education, first of a single people, and then of a spiritual culture, the Church of Christ. Let no one complain about their fate in the world, about the symptoms of mortality, or the false expectations to release from suffering which modern people insist on cultivating in such a luxuriant manner. Human life matters because it matters to God. It has no other dignity or purpose.

Seventy Five

Called to true health

Yesterday was St Luke's day, a commemoration by Christians not only of the Apostle who was a physician but also of the Church's commitment to the ministry of healing. That ministry, however, is now having to be exercised in a context which evaluates health and sickness in a manner radically different from the past: modern Western people assume the collectivization of medicine. The vocation of those attending the sick is no longer influenced by the Christian ideals of self-sacrifice, of learning spiritual lessons through the experience of bodily suffering, of recognizing that men and women are inseparable from the chances and variables, the corrosions and the hazards, to which the laws of the Creation subject all things. Health is now an industry – the largest industry in this country in fact. Public figures and each of us individually refer to it in the language of rights and entitlements. To some extent, in this, we are simply heirs or victims of our own successes in medical advance: our expectations have set themselves upon an unrealistic yet seemingly credible calculation that humanity can always contrive solutions to the ills which afflict it; more funding or more research, or some novel enterprise of planning, will ultimately award society control over physical malfunction or decay. In some degree, indeed, it may. But whatever the palliatives, the tissues will always in the end cease to reproduce themselves satisfactorily, bodies will wear out, immunity will diminish: our advances in medicine will merely have postponed for a few years the inevitability of dissolution, leaving our false expectations searingly unfulfilled. And that is to leave out of account the nasty possibility of horrific new pandemics, to which medicine can bring little relief, either through its own inherent limits or because society does not furnish the high costs involved – as in the AIDS catastrophe of Africa right now.

St Luke is for Christians the prototype of the vocation of healing as a recognition of the lowly place of humanity. The religious tradition of which he is the symbol and patron emphasizes human *love*. It follows the healings of Christ himself, which indicated not entitlements or rights, but divine mercy and the acceptance of divine forgiveness – for our lack of trust in Providence. It was the healed lepers who failed to give thanks for their cure whose behaviour was questioned. The Saviour lived in a society whose people sought a *meaning* in sickness: the answers they gave were often incorrect, through attributing human ailments to personal moral failure, but their instincts were right. Humans are subject to the laws which determine all things; they do not possess what modern people claim as an entitlement, which is exemption from suffering. Christian healing addresses the spiritual nature of each person in a ministry of love, while at the same time using every gift of reason which God gives to advance medical knowledge. We are called to be partners with God in the development of the earth; we are also, however, called to discern spiritual truths in the transient afflictions which, in modern society, are allowed to preoccupy us.

———

Seventy Six

Civic religion

ঠ৩ঙঃ

In the natural process of things it could be expected that the observance of Remembrance, for the dead of the wars of the twentieth century, would gradually diminish. The generations whose lives were personally deeply affected by the sacrifice of relatives and friends are passing away, the circumstances of political reality are now very different. The world changes: who now remembers the dead of the wars of the eighteenth century? No matter how carefully the young are taught about the values of the past they necessarily cease to feel personal involvement with the passions of past events – unless there are vibrant propagandist impulses which make the formulators of opinion in the present world reinvent them to serve modern agendas. Thus teaching the young about the Holocaust is now a regular feature in school programmes: a recent innovation which serves to instil modern sacral values attached to anti-racism. But Remembrance of the lost dead was originally about the concepts of heroism, military valour, and national honour – concepts not obviously prominent in the vision of, let us say, the compilers of national educational curriculae or programme planners of the BBC. So why is the Remembrance observance suddenly so popular, with the young seemingly enthusiastic to perpetuate its existence? Why is it being reinvented, since that is what must be happening if there is, as there is, no evident revival in the ideals of military valour or personal sacrifice?

The explanation is probably to be found in the same kind of popular moral culture which sensationalizes transport accidents or child murders or the deaths of celebrities. We are looking at the emergent values of the post-Christian world, in which people cannot cope with the facts of their own natures. Having set aside the concept of a sovereign Divine Person the people of the modern world worship Humanity, place human welfare above all things, judge crimes against humans to be the most terrible sins imaginable. When human nature exhibits indications of its inherent nastiness – which it actually does all the time – people sensationalize their responses, indulge in extravagances of emotional self-indulgence. Remembering the war dead is becoming part of this general scheme of things; those remembered are now envisaged as violated human lives, not as upholders of values; as the victims of an obscenity, war, and not as the valiant who sacrificed themselves. Remembrance Sunday is being, almost unconsciously, reinvented as a Festival of Humanity. Church services are still the location of these events because there are, as yet, no conventional alternatives. It is just a matter of time before teddy bears as well as flowers are deposited at memorials of the fallen. Modern people indulge in emotional drama to satisfy a disposition in themselves, rather than as a tribute to the dead, when they resort – as they now do in increasing numbers – to services of Remembrance. It is not our emotional needs, however, but gratitude to those who sacrificed themselves which should lie at the heart of this weekend's sad observances.

Seventy Seven

Clarity with truth

ഔ‍ര‍ു

Christianity is being converted, by its own leaders, into an affair of personal selection. Increasingly the faithful are encouraged to see the Faith not as a structure of doctrines, but as a personal quest. Clergy and lay ministers are now trained in the supposition that it will be their vocation to assist their flocks in this work of religious enterprise, putting together an understanding of the message of Jesus suited to personal disposition and emotional requirements. The whole concept that Christianity expresses a fixed body of permanent teaching, which needs to be differently presented in the cultural shifts of each age and place yet which is always the same and is rendered in categories which can be exactly defined, is being abandoned. In its place liberal Christianity proposes an open-ended agenda, fashioned according to personal inclination, whose only fixed point is a reverence for human values. The core message of the Saviour is now being represented as being more or less exclusively a statement of them. It is humanity and its welfare which is the centre of very much modern understanding of Christianity – and a good deal of impatience is now shown in the Church with those who are 'old-fashioned' enough to be unpersuaded by the grand vision. Those whose adhesion to dogma in social teaching, as concerning race equality or gender issues, for example, are dismissive of the entire concept of dogma in religious doctrine.

That is well enough known. What still needs to be emphasized, however, is the class basis of the prevalent mood. A religion whose essence is individual enterprise with ideas is a religion for the educated elite, for the chattering classes, for those whose addictive moralism is amply satisfied by perpetual re-examination of the 'issues' which appear to form the content of modern Christian understanding of applying the message of the Lord. One wonders how the rural poor, who have constituted the membership of the Church for two thousand years, would have managed without a structure of doctrinal teaching to inform their religious senses. Even in these days of universal education the majority of Christian adherents are in countries of the developing world for whom conditions – especially conditions of personal choice – are little different from the Christian past in Europe. In moments of moral decision, and in the daily reference for spiritual guidance, Christianity has always recognized that its truths need to be rendered in accessible and fixed statements. Definition of doctrine is essential in the real world, where ideological difference, even expressed in the simplest language, is permanent and important to the identity of human life. Believing Christians need to know rapidly and clearly what it is they are required to believe. Similarly the devil as a roaring lion seeks whom he may devour: error needs to be recognized so that it may be eschewed, and the soul protected from the pollution of false ideas and mistaken behavioural patterns. The Church must be aware that its teaching function is paramount, and that its truth is adduced collectively, in the consensus of the faithful, and not through private choice.

Seventy Eight

Not counting the cost

ೞಀಚ

The men whom Jesus called to be his disciples were not, by worldly estimation, socially significant, or important, or even remarkable. They were gathered from ordinary work, the kind of people whose experience of life is direct and simple. Today the Church honours the memory of St Andrew, brother of Peter – two of the fishermen who left their nets and followed the Lord. The ministry of Jesus, in fact, was *organized:* he founded a *Church*, with designated leaders – later he sent out seventy others to spread the good news of salvation. People today often seem to suppose that Jesus addressed crowds and moved around randomly in the small towns of Galilee, and periodically travelled, as others did, to the observances at Jerusalem. In reality his time during his ministry, in the last two years or so of his life, was spent in consciously setting up an organization; he taught a *corps* of men, with leaders selected by himself, who were, after his death, to be his body in the world – as their successors are to this day.

It is the ordinariness of those he chose which should most impress us, however. Here were not the clergy of his day, or the educated elite or the movers of opinion, but those whose place in life stands for the generality. The disciples were what most people are like, and they were like us. They were, that is to say, frail in their moral and spiritual capacities: Peter denied Christ when he had the opportunity to witness to him and to demonstrate his loyalty – just as we might. One of those chosen betrayed the Lord to his enemies – as we do when we fail to make Jesus the priority of our choices in daily living. Most, however, become so influenced by the great love of God, which

Christ literally embodied, that they followed him in death, as in the case of Andrew, a martyr's death. Would we do that? Probably not; human faith is fragile, and our self-deception is great. Ponder the kind of excuses, and rationalizations of motives, we settle for when we elect to avoid truly sacrificial conduct. Modern people, in particular, seem to envisage a discipleship of Christ which is all beautiful thoughts and emotional luxuriance – it doesn't include pain or suffering or the choice of courses of belief and action which might disadvantage us or deny us the possibility of that appalling goal of men and women today, 'self-fulfilment'. The modern concept of religion as personal therapy is defective in many ways, but no more searingly than in its rejection of a dimension of personal suffering. The seventy whom the Lord sent out to declare his message were instructed to carry nothing with them – to be dependent on those to whom they were sent. Our world does not value such austerity; our clergy, indeed, regard themselves as inadequately served if they are not provided with the standard issues of the bourgeois lifestyle. But honour St Andrew and those like him who left everything for the love of Jesus.

Seventy Nine

A bleak vision

⅋⅋⅋

Thirty years ago Church leaders in this country, and in Western nations in general, were defining the essentials of the Christian ministry in terms of a critique of political society. The evils of capitalism were extensively dwelt upon, as was the nature of what contemporaries called the 'power-structures'. The spirit of the age envisaged generous quantities of vulgar Marxism – which was generously represented within the Church, though not under that name. There was also the dramatic allure of a species of anarchism, conveyed principally in the remnants of the student movement of the 1960s – to which Church leaders had paid a good deal of pious attention and to which they offered a sympathetic if opaque approval. They were heady days. But where has it all gone? Where, now, may one discern the political scrutiny of the churchmen, once declared to be so central to Christian concerns with the world? Social criticism today appears confined to episodic utterances on the treatment of asylum seekers or to moralistic references to issues of race relations; political discourse seems entirely absent. Is it therefore possible to assume that institutional Christianity in this country is content with capitalism and its motives and effects? Are the liberal secular values of our society to be taken as embodiments of the Gospel – if not, why the silence? There were, thirty years ago, one or two vociferous Christian writers who did, it is true, question the then consensus. They did not dismiss the attempt to discern in Christian teaching a valid and religiously authentic critique of the political and social order but rejected the amateurishness of the bishops' various analyses – and their slavish adhesion to the values and ideas of the secular intelligentsia. They were dispatched to the periphery, where they have remained. How did the leaders, possessed of all the resources of the Church, come to go so silent on these great matters?

There is no very clear answer. It is possible to notice, however, that they have, once again, merely followed the fashions of thought around them. The prevalent tone is now set by the bourgeois liberal reformism of the Blair political culture. The young have ceased to be passionate about politics – as they have in fact about virtually all the great ideas, including religious ones, which have exercised the intelligence of civilized society for nearly three thousand years. What might be called the bishops' 'thought' seems to assume the permanent validity of the concept of the 'plural society': a resignation, that is to say, from public endorsement of any higher end in the life of the state. Political association has become an affair of policing and welfare; apart from a few liberal dogmas about issues of race and gender, and so forth, there appears to be little inclination, in Church or state, to envisage a higher purpose for human life. Once again, then, the Church leaders reflect the spirit of the age, and the age is more godless than ever.

Eighty

Matters of higher importance

ଖ୍ଠଓଔ

It has been usual in the development of society for the exponents of the dominant ideology to employ the authority of the state to propagate and protect their ideas. The state, indeed, has been imagined to exist to promote the educative conditions in which higher ideas can receive a structured representation. These were religious – since the separation of the sacred and the secular is a modern development which, though it seems permanent from a Western liberal perspective, could well prove to be unstable. The re-emergence of Islam as a militant religious ideology committed to the use of the machinery and authority of the state, in a highly advanced and technologically accomplished form, is challenging accepted notions about the inevitability of a link between modernity and secularization. Most Western Christians, however, seem unlikely to abandon their new reluctance to use the coercive power of the state to protect and promote religious ideas. Remaining defenders of the existence of a formal constitutional Establishment of the Church, in fact, usually employ pragmatic defences of their position, and contend for state inclusion of other religious representatives in a fashion which, logically rendered, would vitiate their own grounds for *any* link of Church and state. If the state has the capacity to recognize religious truth and use its authority to promote it, then that truth must have enough explicit content to give the state a means of framing a public polity in which it is expressed. And that requires *exclusion* of the ideas of religious bodies which promote unsuitable beliefs –

polygamy, let us say, or child prostitution (both practices found in some religions in the past). The capacity of public authority to discriminate in such matters is more or less universally recognized in modern liberal societies when it comes to such social-ethical issues as race relations, sexual equality, or policy towards the disabled: here the use of state power to enforce 'correct' opinion is upheld with moral emphasis and well-defined exclusivity. The same Church leaders who these days get very uneasy about the use of state authority to promote the Christian religion are, as it happens, also those who passionately endorse the concept of 'the plural society' and recognition of value diversity to the extent that no religion should be accorded official priority over any other in the governance of society. Thought in these areas is very confused, however. Do they believe that the state should not promote higher ideals, or do they, as many would appear to, imagine that human welfare and 'caring' dispositions are themselves higher ideals – rather than being, as they are, what remains when public authority has given up the promotion of religious truth and has opted, instead, to support ordinary materialism? The future of the unfolding debate about the Establishment of religion in this society should be concerned with effects of a de-consecration of the state, rather than trivial concern over the internal condition of the C. of E.

Eighty One

Bricks without straw

80CB

To be a *member* of the Church of Christ is to be exactly that – in the old meaning of the word member – a link or organic part. As the Church is Christ's body in the world, those who are baptized become the living means by which he is conveyed to each generation of aspirants to salvation; they are the agents of God's will, the means through whom his presence is declared to human understanding. That is why in God's providential scheme humans were 'made in his image': they were accorded, that is to say, the capacity to determine by reason and reflection, through experience of existence on the planet, and through the divine Revelation which God makes of himself, what is the very nature of his will for us. As men and women pass through the changing sequences of human culture they are the bearers of Christ – forever called to determine what is essential and always needs to be observed and interpreted, and what may be discarded as merely the accretion of a particular time or place. This is a collective vocation. Christians are, by definition, those who make this pilgrimage of faith together, engaged in mutual consultation to preserve a common mind about the knowledge of God, and having an agreed voice, also, over what is to be identified as an erroneous development in ideas or practice. There is a necessary universality in the process, since Christian truth is identified by being everywhere the same, both across the measure of present understanding, and in communion with the spiritual understanding of those who have gone before. The body of the Lord is not a debating society or an agency for the execution of enlightened philanthropy; it is the residence of his grace.

What is notable in modern experience, however, is the general ignorance about Christian doctrine both inside and outside the Church. It is also extraordinary to discover how shallow, often, is the knowledge of the Faith disclosed by even the clergy – who are well-acquainted enough with Scripture but unaware of the doctrinal formulations of tradition. Modern people have an inclination to imagine that they are self-sufficient in the means by which they can determine religious ideas for themselves, in isolation from the centuries of faith or the witness of the universal Church. This, it must be repeated, is a characteristic of the worshippers in the pews as much as it is of the external enquirer. Their data for arriving at Christian knowledge now tends to be the available bandwagon of media ethical debate, shunted on to the remnants of once-recognized liturgical vehicles. They make up religion for themselves. The incentive is no longer surrender to Christ's will, as a consequence of his having called them to repentance, but the pursuit of personal meaning or aesthetic sense. Some seek consolation because of bleak experiences of modern social culture. To all, however, the Saviour declares the same invitation: repent, for the Kingdom of God is near. The Church does not exist to be a fellowship of spiritual convenience; it exists to serve Christ's will by teaching his truths. And those truths must first be learned: they are not merely what we believe we want.

Eighty Two

Angels not Anglicans

ಜಿcs

Human sexuality is not given a very great priority in the moral exhortations of the Church today. There is some commentary on the current obsession with child molestation, and a degree of concern with anything which looks as if it may relate to women's rights. The Roman Catholics are more involved than the Protestants with teachings about sexual conduct – a consequence, doubtless, of greater consistency of teaching generally, and reflecting, also, the centralized supervision of the Vatican. Catholics are insistent on the wickedness of abortion; the Anglicans, though formally committed to its condemnation, rarely bring the matter to public attention: the issue is too divisive for the taste of the leadership. But when it comes to routine sexual behaviour, to the daily decisions which people make in relation to the stewardship of their bodies and of the bodies of others, there are now silences when once there was an abundance of advice and moral exhortation. The laity would anyway ignore any teaching they found inconvenient – as the Catholics have discovered over the issue of artificial means of birth control – and the clergy seem either to share their rationalizations or to proclaim libertarian attitudes as 'healthy' and 'normal'. Theologians and Church writers release a torrent of abuse at St Paul, now routinely declared to be the father of puritanism. Everyone in the Church seems terrified of seeming old-fashioned when it comes to sex, and almost two thousand years of accumulated Christian wisdom is lightly discarded by a generation of religious leaders whom one would not in ordinary circumstances trust to remove the wrapper from a convenience food.

The question of sexual conduct, however, is deeply related to one of the most basic roots of Christian teaching. For it concerns the essentials of human nature. If men and women were autonomous creatures, capable of detached rational choices in matters of personal desire, inevitably altruistic in their dealings with others, and perpetually seeking lifestyles which tended to higher purposes, there would be a prospect that their sexual instincts might just always prove benign. But they are not. To suppose that they are is a fair test of materialist Humanism. In reality, as the Church has hitherto insisted, people are corrupted, and stand in need of redemption. That is why the Son of God came into the world. If left to self-selected moral constraints they use their bodies as utilities, and surrender to the impulses of pleasure with scant or no regard for the consequences of their actions – either for their own spiritual formation or for the moral welfare of others. Then the only sanctions are those of personal disadvantage or unhappiness: an unwanted pregnancy, for example, or the social unpleasantness of a discarded sexual partner. Christians, however, know that in linking sexuality to reproduction God dignified the human person in the very act of sexual commission – not a paradox, but an experience of self-fulfilment which confirms the sanctification of our material beings. Humans, nevertheless, endlessly seem to seek their own debasement, and imagine the consequences to be free of moral purpose.

Eighty Three

———

The simplicity of truth

ഇൗരു

Humans are material creatures: they are of the earth, earthy –
as St Paul wrote. They can only know things derived from
experience of the world or observation of the heavens; they are
themselves integrated with the Creation. So God made them,
and their first consciousness of him came naturally, in their
understanding of the world of nature. God then appeared as a
river deity, or a God of the thunder and mountain, or a spirit
dwelling in fissures of the ground, or recognized in the fate of
peoples. Thus the earliest perceptions of the Jewish people,
whose God presided over a folk-wandering, and whose august
presence was seen in a burning bush. And thus also in Fortuna,
the Roman divinity of chance or fate. As understandings of the
Divine implicit in the created order became more educated – or
better observed – God revealed himself directly. He came into
the world, and in Christ made the most perfect disclosure of
his nature, and left humanity, in his body the Church, a means
by which his revealed truth could go on being present to the
understanding of men and women for all time.

In the spiritual landscape, therefore, there is no place for
fantasies, and probably no personal experience of the divine
presence. God is known because he is observable in his works,
and because he comes to us as a person in Jesus – and Jesus is
known through adherence to the teaching of the People of God,
and sacred tradition of the believers, which each Christian
is obliged to transmit to future generations. To be a Christian is
to stand in that company of the bearers of the knowledge
of God. There is no need – and actually no real possibility – of
knowing the Divine through 'paranormal' experience, or by

some suspension of the material laws and processes: as if God worked through magical effusions, or chose particular persons, often extremely unprepossessing ones at that, to be the recipients of special information. Miraculous occurrences surrounded the existence of God himself in the person of Christ, and some of those have attached to the lives of his saints: they are, as it were, localized demonstrations of the creative power of God; evidences, like fragments left behind in the formation of stars, that a creative event has occurred; or perhaps they may resemble the afterglow of sunset in a desert. Religion is about the Divine as the minds of men and women experience the world – their minds were created to interpret only the world of their senses. There is no other way to know God, and this is the only means available for us to communicate with him.

Yet we live in an age in which there is an increasing disposition to seek personal experiences of the Divine. They are deceptions. 'After-Death Experiences' following bodily trauma, like supposed abduction by aliens, relate ideas already formed by popular culture and its images. Recreational hallucinogenic drugs evoke the same sensations. The movement of the emotions is simply a contrivance dependent for meaning on preceding cultural conditioning. The religion of Jesus does not need to be delivered by such means. For it is about a person who brought us all the knowledge of God. We have only to look to him.

Eighty Four

Accumulating unrighteousness

ဆၢငၢ

At the centre of Christianity are two statements about ourselves: that we are sinners, and that we are capable of forgiveness. Both are received with insufficient seriousness in the modern world. Sin really does attach to each person in the very nature of their beings; it seeps into their motives, their behaviour, their understanding of their capabilities. God came into the world in order to save us from our *sin:* therein is the reality behind the purpose and the sacrificial death of Jesus. At the beginning of the day every Christian soul, each person who aspires to redemption, should recognize that it is his personal failings which procured the Crucifixion. In view of our liability to blame others for the wretchedness of human conduct, of the ordering of social existence, and of our persistent tendency to expend our time on earth in trivial concerns, and the pursuit of security, this is a solemn matter indeed. And yet the God who died at Calvary offered individual salvation, and it is available simply through personal repentance. For that is the measure of the great love of God; not that we loved him, but that he loved us. We are called, as St Francis Xavier expressed it in his lovely mission prayer, not to love God because of any hope of heaven but because God loved us. It is a truth never taken seriously enough. Sin, therefore, is neutralized by the offer of forgiveness. It is not that – because of our spiritual frailty and the inherent corruption of our natures – we are ever going to cease from wrongdoing and wrong beliefs, but that the divine gift of forgiveness nevertheless admits us to eternal life despite ourselves. How much greater is the greatness of God's love than anything we can contrive! There is, however, a condition annexed to redemption.

It is mentioned in the Lord's own Prayer: we ask to be forgiven *as we ourselves forgive others.* The universal fellowship of the corrupt is to be redeemed by universal forgiveness. Humans find that extremely difficult to achieve, and are constantly contriving excuses – some with extensive intellectual pedigrees – to avoid delivery. Yet God calls us individually to the forgiveness of our neighbour. The modern world seems set to increase, rather than diminish, the mismatch between Christian aspirations and human performance in this whole area of mutual forgiveness. The first sign of this seems to be in the demonizing of people who have committed acts of wickedness which society is conditioned to loathe so much that they are regarded as outside of human forgiveness. Thus the fate of sex offenders, or racists. Indeed the catalogue of zero forgiveness has now extended from actual commission to wrong thought – as they have discovered who download unsocial material from computers, and have found their lives broken by an expanding criminal code. The new puritanism of our age is exactly like the moral intolerance of the past: it is linear, unforgiving, and popular. Listen to the spiralling debate about crime and punishment, and behold the rising tariffs of custodial punishment, and you will perceive what a world slipping away from the practice of forgiveness is like.

Eighty Five

The cost of discipleship

ॐ

Christianity is very demanding. The believer is asked to make enormous self-sacrifices, and to surrender to the sovereignty of a God whose claims are exclusive and whose laws are often in direct contradiction of what may seem most desirable to the individual. In an age which lays huge emphasis on *human* rights and entitlements, and on liberal choice in beliefs and lifestyles, the follower of Jesus is presented with non-negotiable commandments: the citizens of the Kingdom of Christ are to give up some of their most comfortable and cherished practices and ideas and to conform to the pattern of sacrificial living exemplified in the life of the Saviour himself. People today want religion to be all about personal consolation, beautiful tableaux of idealized human relationships, emotional satisfaction; to be a kind of summary of the sacral values of surrounding society. But the religion of Jesus actually goes against the grain. It begins, as Jesus in his earthly ministry began, by calling each person to repentance – to remind each of inherent depravity; that humans are liable to wickedness, not simply in grand choices or courses of action, but in daily exchanges and lost opportunities of authentic altruism and service. Modern people have a great measure of difficulty in grasping the essential fact that religious belief, far from being the comforting and emollient culture of sentiment they seek, is in reality both exacting and disagreeable. It is against the corrupted nature of men and women to sur-render to Jesus, and the love he holds out to them, to be fruitful and effective, needs to be matched by their response. It *hurts* to be religious; it is necessary to close so many doors we would rather keep open, and so many things which give us pleasure turn out to be contrary to laws which God himself has established for his creatures. The modern world, of course, is very adept at insisting that those laws are in reality mere human inventions; many Christians are themselves these days inclined to argue that they are just misunderstandings made by their predecessors in the Faith. But the plain and ordinary meaning of the words used by Christ himself in his teaching are not ambiguous. Whoever would follow him, he declared, must give up even family loyalties in order to take up the Cross.

From this it must seem strange to have to turn to the inclination of Church leaders today to present their understanding of religion as if it required the mechanics of market forces. Reduced to an affair of social camaraderie, and packaged for its emotional attractiveness, the love of God is represented as a product available without personal cost. The notion that Christianity is actually a structure of doctrines, which makes exclusive claims upon the will of the believer, is plainly incompatible with a culture which expects religion to comprise indiscriminate niceness. Generalities are so much more easily accepted than precise articles of belief – especially among people whose chief object in life would appear to be the pursuit of mere happiness. Authentic religious belief induces pain; true serenity, true joy, comes from obedience.

Eighty Six

The faith of sinners

$\mathcal{EO}\mathcal{CB}$

It is probably the example given by Christians themselves which most puts people off adherence to the Faith. Reasonably enough, observers expect that those attempting to model their lives on the teaching of Christ will achieve something approximate to spiritual formation – that their conduct, that is to say, will show some dissimilarities with the standards of the world, that the public will find them admirable as exemplars of the divine love in action. It is not only in the modern world, but often in the past, that scandals have attached to Christians whose moral conduct has shown regrettable features. Today, much publicity is given to clergy guilty of the sexual abuse of minors; in the nineteenth century it was the popular demonology of the secret passions of nuns which excited a virulent Protestant disgust. In both cases the outrage over lack of purity provoked disillusionment with Christianity as a religion. As support for church attendance declines still further, the sample of those who actually constitute the institutional presence of the Church in society becomes progressively less representative of society generally; and what very commonly describes the tiny gutterings in the pews is not sanctity of life or consistency of spiritual understanding but, to express it bluntly, a weird introspection which takes the form of a closed society. Hypocrisy, however, remains the chief charge against religion in the judgement of the popular culture: Christians are not perceived to act in a manner which is any more elevated than the going rate.

But that, as it happens, is exactly what the religion of Jesus is all about. The Lord whose supreme concern for his creatures

led him to visit the earth and to die in expiation of their sins –
the Lord whose Ascension was celebrated this week – was
precisely a lover of sinners, of the child molesters and the
degraded. The Church exists, as his body in the world, in order
to perpetuate his message of forgiveness. It was meant to be the
place where those who are too weak to live moral lives can find
refuge, and those whose breaches of convention offend the
niceness of the nice people. There is, it is true, a problem when
the level of *intellectual* discernment gets too low among
believers, and when Christians themselves are incapable of
achieving a sound understanding of the nature of their own
faith – a characteristic in our own time, perhaps, as much of the
clerical leadership as of the led. What that probably indicates,
however, is that the Faith first delivered to fishermen has been
intellectualized into the wrong categories by those who are too
approximate in sympathy to modern secular culture to be
capable of seeing the wood for the trees.

So rejoice at the glory of the Ascension: the Lord departs from
the world in majesty in order to be present with it in the least
worthy of his creatures. To the eye of the unperceptive the
believers of today may appear careless or inattentive to their
highest calling; to Jesus, on the other hand, they are the poor in
the endowments of the world for whom he came.

Eighty Seven

Spiritual selfishness

଼ଠୠଔୠ

There is no lack of commentary about the improvident manner in which the resources of the planet are being used up. There are a few, largely token, attempts at conservation and rationing, a number of substitutions of materials and energy supplies; in general, however, society goes on living far beyond its means of providing resources for the future, and everyone simply hopes that our successors will develop new means of solving our problems. We hand them a depleted legacy while we claim the benefits of material profligacy for ourselves. Similarly, the present generation of Christians treat their religious life as a utility. They squander the deposit of faith inherited from the past as if they had no responsibilities for the knowledge available to future believers. They treat Christianity as a personal benefit – a spiritual commodity which exists, so they would seem to imply, for their personal emotional needs, and for the satisfaction of their individual disposition to seek aesthetic sensation or therapeutic support. The sense that the Faith is the transmission of the living body of Christ himself, and that to enter into it is to share his suffering as the essential preliminary to receiving his glory, scarcely enters into the consciousness of most modern Christians. What they want to experience is instant fellowship, or, perhaps, a higher confirmation of their adhesion to the ethical priorities of the moment. The religion of Jesus is no longer perceived as a body of teaching, precise and revealed, but as a sensation for emotional gratification. It is, accordingly, being used up. By becoming absorbed by personal need it leaves little to transmit: we make religious truth depend upon the nature of our consumption, we brand it as though it was like any other consumable – different only in that it serves needs that we imagine we cannot satisfy in other ways. Modern people, that is to say, are immersed in thoroughly material living, sharing many of the materialist attitudes of the times, and then add religious 'belief' as a sort of extra layer or dimension. Christians today should stop in their tracks and ask the simple question, 'what am I doing to pass on the message of Jesus to my successors?' And it will not do, if a future of spiritual understanding is to be realized, simply to equate the Christian message with the liberal-Humanist agenda of the day – which is what the Church leaders tend to do. What is needed, by each Christian soul, is a spiritual audit in which the duty of faith is recognized as involving repentance of sin, amendment of life, and surrender to the demands of God.

Instead, we use up the treasures of spirituality on ourselves and leave little for the future. The nature of our consumption means that we add little to help to create a deposit for the future. In an age of management, poverty of ideology, and manipulation of opinion, Christians are well placed to offer the world a crucial example of fidelity to tradition. So far they do not appear to be notably conscious that their actions actually move them in the reverse direction. What is needed is a call to the Holy Spirit – the One in whom all truth is guaranteed. It is what Whitsun is all about.

Eighty Eight

Penetrating reality

☙⊗Ꮬ

In the ancient world, when the imaginative and intellectual dispositions existed which determined the way in which Western religious traditions have developed, the division of social reality into the sacred and the secular – which we now take for granted – had not occurred. Nor did people envisage the material world as supplying explanations which were significantly different in kind from what they thought of as the world routinely visited by the gods. In Greek thought the universal categories of understanding were embodied in the religious myths – giving a superstructural semblance of polytheism to divine truths which in fact represented human perceptions about general characteristics. Thus the gods were allocated specialist functions or territorial domains: there were divinities of love, or fate, or war, and so forth. What they personified, in a literal sense, were truths about the nature of the world and of human creatures. In the Jewish religion, the will of God was known through the agency of actual events; the general was made particular in the experience of a single people who gradually came to recognize transcendent values in the progressive unfolding of historical drama. Everywhere the communion of gods and men was through intermediaries. God spoke through oracles and cultic practices in the Greek understanding, and through prophets and sacred writings in the Jewish. Christianity evolved from a synthesis of both modes. It was thoroughly Jewish in theological expectations and it became deeply Greek in the manner of its doctrinal formulation in the early Councils of the Church. This latter process was helped because of the degree to which Judaism had itself become Hellenized in the two centuries before Christ's birth. Humans can only conceive God in the images and vocabulary supplied by the world of material experience. But Christianity appeared at a time when the Divine was accessible through traditions of thought and reflection – and through the immediacy of the human need of social and moral cohesives – which recognized no division between the will of God and the physical creation. When Christians formulated the doctrine of the Holy Trinity, which they celebrate tomorrow, they were attempting to express a sublime truth in a manner which resonated with this general scheme of things. The God who created order may be known about through the Personalizing of *three* forms in which he has made himself apparent to his creatures. The Father, the Son, and the Holy Spirit, like the diversities of holiness expressed in the mythical beings of the Greek world, are three representations of a unity. They are present to men and women, however, not in fables but in direct effusions of the divine presence.

Modern people have no sense of any of this. To them the sacred exists to add some transcendent dimension to lives which otherwise are more or less wholly claimed by secular priorities. They don't really want to know about the nature of God – only what he will do for them. Yet to know about him is to know, also, about human insufficiency and corruption. The glory of the Trinity is the vision of a divine reality which is so vastly greater than ourselves and our trivial needs.

Eighty Nine

Another way

ԒᎠᏟᏒ

The new millennium has started off in characteristic fashion: men and women are beset by fear. Not only in the greater perspective of world events, and the wars and rumours of wars that are familiar enough in the human record, but in daily life. Just at a time when scientific and technological advance has relieved people of many afflictions which their predecessors actually regarded as inseparable from normality, they are more fearful of dislocation to their lives than ever. It is partly a matter of changing the goalposts. As in ideas, so in daily material existence: there is an escalating progression of expectations whose ultimate standard is set by a completely painless existence. Whether it is a matter of social welfare provision or an explanation of the universe, people have now come to regard perfection of achievement as a kind of birthright, and virtually anything that falls short of it either the basis of grievance or an incentive to spend more in the belief that anything can be made accessible given a rational use of resources. Fear, however, feeds upon itself. Modern people have become victims of their own fears, and are – as Pope John Paul II pointed out early in his pontificate – becoming imprisoned within their own creations. It is the endless pursuit of security which is to blame; the sense that life owes us repose and the satisfaction of material desires. When the latter, even to these blinkered luminaries, seems to pall, there is always, now, the addition of a 'spiritual dimension' – by which is usually meant some provision of aesthetic sensation, an imagined dignifying of the individual by immersion in pools of emotional manipulation. Modern people also own so much. Many of their fears relate to the possible loss of their property, that moth and rust will corrupt, or that thieves will break through and steal. They are, additionally, terrified of insecurity in their 'relationships'. Having removed mutual obligations, and duty owed to God's laws from their world-picture, men and women seek relations with others which have a high level of ordinary hedonism within the motivation. It is the problem of perfection again. When their partner cannot deliver, things fall apart.

All this is in very great contrast to the Christian way. Those who try to follow Christ are dedicated to a large measure of self-denial, both materially and emotionally. For them, life in society is not primarily about securing personal advantages; they are not in thrall to a scramble to hold on to what is possessed. Nor do they seek to possess the persons of others, whether in 'relationships' or in the social nexus generally, Christians educate their desires, and try to create priorities in their manner of living, and in their expectations, which are intended to mould them into creatures of transcendence. They make themselves, that is to say, aspirants to eternal life, and seek the consecration of their beings with graces which they cannot earn but which Christ himself freely gives to those who ask. It is what life is for.

Ninety

The sin of first resort

ᏕᎧ

For very many modern people, both inside the Church and outside of it, religious belief is losing any effective connection with personal discipline. They see Christianity as a matter of personal explanation – as a way of dignifying themselves and their existence, as a series of beautiful emotional sensations, as a progression to some kind of social camaraderie, and sometimes, even, as an asset in stabilizing relationships with other people. But the notion that religion is essentially about submission to the laws of God, and that those laws often conflict with our natural inclinations, does not have much appeal. The whole idea, in fact, that *natural* feelings can in anyway be hostile to benign human intentions is not in favour: there is now no general acceptance of Original Sin, no sense that humanity exists in a condition of inherent depravity from which only the special and supervening grace of God can bring release – and even then not from the dreadful things which we do but from the spiritual consequences. The purpose of life is judged to be pleasure, and anything that impedes its achievement is considered an evil. So the understanding of the Divine nature is itself reinterpreted, and 'God' is reassembled for human hedonism, in modern moral understanding, as a being of indiscriminate acceptance of human self-seeking. The sins of the modern world relate to uncaring attitudes or imperfect appreciation of humanity's claims to rights. It is only a few who persist in regarding human life as requiring discipline and mortification, and who consider the service of God as involving abstinence from very many things to which our natures incline us.

Issues of human sexuality show this in a particularly clear manner. For in almost no other area of human experience has the pursuit of pleasure been emancipated from moral consideration with such decisiveness. There is much talk about 'caring attitudes' towards others inside 'relationships'; this, however, largely amounts to empty declamation. The essential fact is that people are coming to regard their bodies as utilities, the vehicles of pleasurable sensations, and the moral boundaries are determined not by reference to external (least of all to divine) laws, but by the degree of reciprocal pleasure derived from sexual commission by the partners. If nobody gets hurt it's all right. Such a moral vision, despite its crude banality, lurks somewhere in much modern liberal moral theology. The sages of the Church share the conviction, widespread in modern society, that the fewer restrictions on sexual practice the better. And so centuries of acquaintance with human realities, and the accumulated wisdom of the ages, is overturned in order to acclaim 'healthy' attitudes to sexuality. The dark side of our natures always reappears, however, and then people are left without guidance or solace.

Ninety One

Fallen standards

ᚸᚲᚷ

The Church has a problem with its moral theology which it chooses, characteristically, to set aside. It is quite simply this: its teaching conveys some extremely clear rules about sexual conduct, applicable to its own members – if no longer prescribed for society in general – which are in plain conflict with the modern collection of liberal Humanist attitudes known as political correctness. Christianity can only be defined by what it has always been, and it does, in consequence, prohibit adultery, serial marriage, sexual relations outside the marriage discipline, various types of deviant acts and excess common in the pagan world in which the early Church was set, and abortion. Some acts need to be defined with precision in order to make sure that what the Church has always rejected was actually *them* and not excesses associated with some of their adherents – homosexuality probably falls into this category – not wrong in itself, but wrong when its practitioners behave in a manner incompatible with Christian teaching. The Church requires its adherents, who are, after all, the body of the Lord in the world, to behave in accordance with its teachings. And there are standards which are applicable across the board. Thus excesses are excesses, whether they are practised by heterosexual or by homosexual people: God made men and women what they are, through the conditioning of the material world of his Creation. Advocates of liberal attitudes to homosexuality within the Church, for example, are liable to condone all excesses characteristic of liaisons and practices within the modern homosexual subculture. Yet adhesion to Christianity involves personal moral discipline of the sort always required of heterosexual relationships. Promiscuity is a betrayal of the dignity which God gives to his creatures, and the denial of transcendent effects in sexual congress, and so is a grave sin. Promiscuous behaviour should be no part of a Christian life, whatever the sexuality or orientation of the believer. The Church's rules in human relationships of all sorts are *meant* to be restrictive; the sad facts of our corrupted natures require no less for our advance in sanctification.

But political correctness posits moral diversity. Within its canons – which are paradoxically very exclusive and intolerant of variations – sexual diversity has a special place of honour. The regulatory machinery of modern government no longer allows discrimination on grounds of sexual preference in an ever-widening area of public life. The leaders of the Church would appear to agree with this – and the bishops, let it be remembered, are still legislators in the half-reformed House of Lords. Do they imagine there is one set of standards applicable in secular society, to which they give their assent, and another, suitable for Church believers, to which they also give their assent? They do not say. Yet there can be no doubt that Christians are called to obey the moral laws the Church has always taught, for that is an essential part of their identity as the earthly representatives of Christ himself.

Ninety Two

Morals off the screen

ಐൠ

It used to be supposed that changes in the moral climate took decades to occur. Ideas filtered down from whichever opinion makers were possessed of social influence; or they were imposed by those charged with social control who had the confidence or the capacity to determine public attitudes. The introduction of mass education initially made little change here, since the content of the education, and the surviving social deference of the recipients, secured a continuing measure of stability. Moral ideas and moral practice are not, anyway, in a precise correlation: statistics of illegitimate births from preceding centuries, when moral declamation was universally adverse, indicate a gap between prescribed teaching and human practice. But moral change was slow and ordered: it took a very long time for what was conventionally acceptable to change – witness the stigma attached to divorce only fifty years ago.

Now that has all changed. The reason is to be sought not so much in the collapse of institutional religion, or in the moral incoherence of the Western liberal intelligentsia – whose ideals have no discernible philosophical basis – so much as in the means now available for the dissemination of ideas of all sorts. It is due to the power of television. Ideas and moral precept are abstract; the nightly presentation, in dramas and 'analysis' of public events by selected experts, is not. Both on the screen and in the classroom a version of unstructured Humanism would seem to prevail: moral virtue is determined by whatever current educated opinion deems conducive to modern canons of politically correct ideas. Soaps are extremely effective means of conveying moral propaganda, modern morality plays which link day-to-day developments in particular lives – lives which are, as in the entertainments of the past, to be followed or avoided, according the assigned roles in the tension of good and evil. The great difference from the past is that there is now *so much* entertainment that it is immediately available, and that it falls upon people with no other source of moral exhortation. The heroes are the tolerant, common-sense moralists who ostensibly respect all viewpoints and decry 'old-fashioned' moralists with their outmoded restrictions. The demons are those practitioners of whatever, for the moment, attracts public obliquity – paedophiles, drug users, racists, or whatever. There is morality without a moral pedigree, a post-Christian assemblage of attitudes dependent for their authority on media promotion. Their dissemination illustrates the permanence of 'false-consciousness': the nightly transfer from the television screen is to those who believe they are 'thinking for themselves'. Moral attitudes can be changed with astonishing rapidity, nothing seems stable – only the rhetoric of caring and 'recognition of diversity' in which it is all received. There is not much point in referring to the Church leaders for permanence, either, since their moral advice would appear to derive from the same source. And when there is a conflict (as over divorce, or sex outside marriage) they keep silent.

Ninety Three

Loyalty to truth

ഇൻരു

Christians today, and those seeking to understand the Christian faith, tend to regard religion as a matter of individual agreement. They examine the evidence, survey the behaviour of Christians in the past and in the present, and assess the extent to which belief would seem to be compatible with modern knowledge about the nature of reality. Many have come to express this exercise in the image of a journey. It is, in fact, a very ancient image; but in the past the journey was a progression through the perils of the world, with its temptations and sorrows, towards the fixed point of the celestial city. In today's understanding the journey is conceived as one of discovery, and the journey of faith is recognized to be a progression through the world in which the aspirant to religious belief picks up the content as he goes along. This is necessarily a highly personal enterprise – as is encouraged by the presentation of religion in school curricula and in such media discussions of religion as exist. The individual person 'discovers' faith in their own needs, and especially in their emotional needs. Religion is imagined as catering to the emotions, whereas 'real data' about the world can be got from secular knowledge. Religion, because centred in emotional satisfaction in this way, is also seen as a means of social integration, or as a way of making each person better fitted to conduct mature relationships with others. This is a world-centred conception of the faith, a projection of personal understanding. But Christianity is not about *understanding* at all: it is about *assent*.

To be a Christian is not to be satisfied that the individual is enhanced in life-skills or that personal significance has been assured; it is to be integrated with the body of Christ in the world – to be his body, in company with others, in time and in eternity, who have surrendered to his call. This is not an exercise in emotional satisfaction or personal fulfilment; it is, on the contrary, to give up individual desires or claims in order to be received into something external to each person – to accept Christ. The Church has a process of *initiation*: baptism. When carried out for very young children, baptism involves promises made on behalf of the infant, who is then reared in a spiritual culture in which the acceptance of Christ has already been determined, and only awaits confirmation in adult life. But baptism is always initiation; the initiate, just as in the mysteries of the ancient world, *assents* to a set of beliefs – he does not try to make them up for himself. To be part of the body of the Lord in the world is to be the agent of his truth; it is *his* truth, not our individual construction of it, that Christians are called to proclaim. God gave reason to men and women in order that they should derive meaning from the world of their experience. They use it, too, to explain the Faith. But the Faith which they explain is not their own possession, for it belongs to the Lord who gave it, and who, amazingly, loved his creatures so much that he died for them.

Ninety Four

The sound of music

‮ЯᏟᏃ‬

Human emotions are not creative, they do not inspire or convey actual messages about reality. What they are is more basic and less articulate; they are firing mechanisms, the triggers of sensation. In this sense the disposition to lust is no different in kind from that which inspires appreciation of great art – both operate to move the individual to recall prior conditioning, the recollection of acquired knowledge, which then supplies satisfaction. Emotions are neutral impulses; they can evoke nothing that is not already within the mind. There can be no sense, therefore, in which music can inform the person about higher truths, or art inspire data not available by other means. Emotions are certainly real enough, and have the advantage of being within everyone's experience. They are not, however, a source of new knowledge; they illustrate sensations with knowledge of which the individual was already possessed.

Today is St Cecilia's day, the patron of music, whose tomb may still be visited in the Catacomb of St Callixtus in Rome. Music has the capacity to inspire emotional response in a manner perhaps more intense than the other arts – as the ancient Greeks knew, when they accorded it a high place in schemes of education. But they did not fall into the error, as we now do, of imagining that music has, of itself, a message to convey. In the modern world an appreciation of music is routinely described as a characteristic of 'spirituality', and many Christians suppose it capable of evoking the presence of the Divine. They are mistaken. What it does is to move the indivual to make associations of the mind, to illustrate existing knowledge, supposedly of higher truths, to which the person has been exposed in the complicated earthly processes of socialization. This is a useful service, and music is rightly cultivated as an adjunct to whatever values the individual adopts. But that is all it does. The Church offers up its praises to God with music – as God's people in the Old Testament did – because music is the best means available to offer to God the finest representations of truth that men and women can contrive. Drugs, too, are only capable of reordering, or dredging up, what is already in the mind, and, like the arts, they are in themselves of neutral value – what they do depends on what they elicit from the human brain. The widespread confusion between aesthetic appreciation and spirituality which is characteristic of modern society is a snare. It encourages people in believing that mere emotional stimulation provides authentic insights into transcendent realities. But it's just a form of entertainment, and whether its effects are beneficial or baneful is entirely dependent upon other values which are already in the mind. So honour St Cecilia and the muse; what she offers, however, she offers to God, and that is what we should do with her gift.

Ninety Five

Seeing ourselves as we are

Christianity is not about the great 'issues' of human society: it is about people. Jesus began his ministry by calling men and women to individual repentance. Certainly their sinful behaviour sometimes took collective forms, and the need for 'applications' of Gospel truths in actual social organization was undoubted; but the primary fault lay within each person. There is an inherent liability to wrong thought and wrong behaviour in everybody, a gravitational downward pull which introduces flaws to our highest and most altruistic intentions. The world will not be put right by the efforts of men – the universality of sin is permanent. This is implicit in the remarks of Jesus about having the poor always with us, and about not becoming absorbed by the cares of the world. Most human evil is not disclosed in dramatic and historic events – acts of genocide, or institutionalized injustice, for example – but in the daily commission of malicious acts or the failure to respond to the needs of others whom we encounter in personal relationships. What is wrong with humanity is out of all proportion to our capability of self-correction. Education has not elevated human goodness or diminished the evil of humanity: it has merely broadened the area of knowledge touching the things we make wrong decisions about. Humans were created by God in order to share with him the progressive development of the planet; they were given lordship over the earth, and left with the freedom of choice to do what they will. The record indicates that, despite their impressive inventiveness, and their discoveries about the nature of the Creation, they have shown themselves completely incapable of eradicating – even of controlling – their inherent corruption. In the growing Humanist and materialist culture of our own times, when self-esteem is regarded as virtuous, and the unilateral declaration of human entitlement is sovereign, there is little sympathy for the notion, central in Christianity, that individual people are described by their sin.

There are many in the modern Church who have come to associate core Christianity with 'issues' in public policy. Their religion is a busy and outraged affair of attending to the various ills to which they regard society as given; their sense is of campaigners joining with secular opinion to secure reforms in which evil is eliminated. But the world will always be full of evil because people are evil. We aspire to virtue, yet our natures are not changed, even after the most radical adoption of religious faith. What is changed by accepting the call of Christ is our relationship to him: Christians are the forgiven. The Lord came into the world not to transform our natures, or to remove our freedom to do evil; he came to offer forgiveness. And the forgiven have the obligation to seek out the service of their brothers and sisters, and this will necessarily, in the circumstances of modern life, take a collective as well as an individual form. Sin remains, however, as the primary condition of humanity, and we should never forget it.

Ninety Six

Knowing the Lord

ଓଠ୍ୟ

The first duty of the Christian life is getting to know Jesus: in his person is to be found the message of God in the world, the most perfect representation of life itself, the way of salvation. But how can we be sure that what we understand about Jesus is true? Some have supposed that after two thousand years all we can discern is the faint echo of his voice; others have claimed a very precise knowledge, purporting to rest on some kind of direct spiritual experience. For believers in the main tradition of the historic Churches, however, the Lord is known collectively – for they constitute, now, his body in the world. The record of his teachings in the writings of the New Testament is the work of men, and so is the interpretation of that record made in each age, by people of very different cultural associations. The solemn truth about Christianity is that the message of Jesus, and a knowledge of him, is what the believers say it is at any given time in history. The remarkable thing about the Church is not that it has survived numerous internal upheavals caused by differences of interpretation, but that the core areas of agreement are so many. For this to be so in the future, however, there must be a sense among the believers that interpreting the person of Jesus is not an individual enterprise, and it does not rest upon personal receipt of intimations of the Divine. The Church as the body of Christ must have the unity of an organic body; it is one and undivided by definition. This is not an aspiration – that is the imagining of Protestant enthusiasts for ecumenism. The Church is undivided *now*, by definition. Where there is essential agreement about the nature of Christ, there is the Church. Liberals tend to envisage the Church as a kind of open debating society. But authentic membership of the Church, though it certainly involves the re-statement of the Faith within the cultural expectations of each age, is essentially about assent to an understanding of Christ that has been reached in the past, and developed in the present, whose authenticity derives from the consensus of all believers. This sounds difficult to achieve: but it exists. Christians call it loyalty to apostolic tradition.

Each Christian is therefore reminded that interpreting the Faith is not a matter of personal selection, nor is it the addition of whatever passing ideals the enthusiasms of the encompassing secular culture may espouse or promote. And it is certainly not the deletion of ancient ideas, carried within the deposit of faith, because the images or language in which they are expressed seem antipathetic to modern ideology. The Faith needs to be reinterpreted in certain particulars – this is always the case – but it never needs to be changed. It is not possible to change the person of Jesus, who came into the world to bring the message of salvation, and whose love for us is as unchanging as it has ever been.

Ninety Seven

The life that is death

ꝏCꙄ

In a materialist culture people tend to define themselves in terms of their material possessions, or their ability to acquire access to services and facilities which enhance, as they suppose, the quality of life. When this is combined with materialist philosophy – in however an inarticulate form – life itself, having no reference beyond the limits of physical existence, becomes at the disposal of the individual, subject to whatever constraints organized society may impose. Humans are notably adaptable, and there is no inherent bias within them to seek transcendent explanations of reality: the supposition that there is (as some Christians seem to contend) derives from human invention. It is itself of cultural origin. People can quite readily exist without higher explanations of human existence, as the state of present liberal society in Western countries, since the decay of organized religious belief began, illustrates well. But then fear sets in. Those who define themselves in relation to their possessions are terrified of losing them; those who see physical existence as all there is become eaten up by worries about their health. The 'health and safety' public culture of our own day is born of these fears – amply lubricated by lawyers waiting in the wings of life's dramas to pick up fees when blame can be apportioned for particular dislocations. Men and women are victims of their own insecurities. One strange by-product is their desire for longevity – presumably because they wish to postpone the one personal phenomenon, death itself, which is always going to be outside their control. So they worry about the means of staying alive longer; and, as if in a divine comedy, the longer they live the less purpose and the more pain there is in

193

their existence. Modern people are miserable creatures: having dethroned God in his heavens, and having sought to usurp his powers to create an earthly paradise, they are constantly mistaking their ancient greed for sophisticated novelty. It is not knowledge which enhances the quality of human life, but wisdom.

Christians know that the gravest of all sins is the failure to trust in Providence. It is God who supplies all that we need for the fullness of life. He calls us, it is true, to a dynamic role in the development of life – to medical discovery, to improved means of food supply, to all the processes by which the resources of the earth may enrich the lives of his creatures. The Bible itself describes how men and women were invited to a lordship over the world and its gifts. Instead, however, of seeking an exploitation of resources which is related to an understanding of the ultimate calling of humanity, men have recklessly pursued untutored self-interest. Occasionally, in today's world, they shed a token tear of compassion for those left behind in the scramble for material living – and this is usually represented as some kind of higher morality. But mostly they are limited by the dimensions of the trough, fearful that it will empty itself.

Ninety Eight

Xmas cheer

ജ

Sacrificial giving is, by definition, giving that hurts. It is a great Christian vocation – actually an indispensable dimension of individual spiritual formation. Whether it is the gift of time, or of money and resources, or of an accomplishment, giving, if it derives only from excess, is a poor thing indeed. Jesus commended the woman who gave all she had, and who, by implication, trusted in Providence to supply her own needs. Modern society is greatly given to token giving, the allocation of excess, both individually in donations to charities or to the Church, and collectively, as when the state determines the level of its overseas aid. Giving today is not sacrificial, and it often has, in fact, distasteful qualities of mere tokenism about it. This is the season of giving. Presents exchanged between relatives and friends at Christmas are just a ritualized remnant, of little moral meaning – except, perhaps, as expressions of real love when they are given, as by really poor parents to their children, in order to prevent their exclusion from the general superfluous distribution. Charitable giving – and this is the most important time of the year for that, too – is rarely sacrificial: allocations are made by institutions because it is expected of them, and although it would be tasteless to enquire into the motives of individual donors there can be little doubt that few who give do so in a manner which involves personal sacrifice. This is not to denigrate their intentions or their virtue; it is simply to point to the fact that charitable donation has ceased to be an exercise in personal formation. It has become, on the contrary, a conventional palliation of the promptings of the conscience – good in itself, useful to the recipients, but not *hurting* the giver.

God did not send the poor and the distressed into this world in order that they should continue in their poverty and distress. Nor did he order societies structured so that those with ample means of living in comfort should continue to do so. The parables of Jesus often depict simple acts of human goodness in which moral exchange involves *pity*: the father had pity for the prodigal son, the good Samaritan took pity on the injured traveller, and so forth. Sometimes in today's rhetoric pity has a kind of patronizing resonance; but it should not be so. Authentic Christian pity is directly linked with action, and true charity has no restraint. What is done is what is needed to achieve real change in the fate of the beneficiary. The Samaritan said he would, on return, pay the full costs of medication. In the Christian life the pursuit of charitable giving should be collective as well as individual. Christians are called to support initiatives in which structural (that is to say, political) solutions are found to assist those in need, throughout the world, or to eliminate the causes of their distress. The means of doing this always involves divisive debate: so be it – engagement with the world, like charity itself, involves personal cost. It is what we are here to do.

Ninety Nine

———

A New Year resolution

ಜಿ೦ಜ

Christians should not get too exercised over news and current affairs. Of all people, they are those who have the perspective of eternity within which to observe and to evaluate the affairs of men. There is very little in the world which is new, and a good deal which is simply the current version of all the ancient errors to which human life is given. It is almost trite to say this: it still needs saying. Christians pore over newspapers and are shocked and scandalized by the evidence they read there of human frailty and human arrogance, of stupidity and cruelty. But they should know that men and women are corrupted: that is why Jesus came into the world – to call them to repentance, to save their souls. In acts of 'prophecy', as they would consider them, however, Christians fall upon news items, and derive opinions which, though in general precisely the same as those of the secular analysts around them, they take to be applications of the Gospel. In the 1960s and 1970s their predecessors scraped together the same fetid remnants of public debate, and identified their enterprise as 'learning from the secular'. The wise observer of human folly realizes he has seen it all before, however, and in the new year which lies before him he will see it all again.

Reading the signs of the times in the passing events, as good Pope John XXIII used to remind Christian people, requires a firmly secured point from which to judge them. Modern liberal thought does not really have one – and even if it did there is no reason to suppose (rather the reverse in fact) that it would correspond with a Christian understanding of reality. The Christian position from which the world's events may be judged begins with the sovereignty of God. It is God's will that human society exists at all, and it is human rebellion against God which provides the occasions for evil. To understand the events of the world it is therefore necessary to understand the nature of God and the order he has set up in his Creation – and that means starting with Church tradition and Holy Scripture. As everybody knows, you can prove virtually anything you want to from Scripture, and nothing is less convincing, at least to a mind educated in wisdom, than simply finding texts which appear to support attitudes adduced from current debate. Interpreting Scripture and tradition is a collective exercise; it is only properly performed when the whole body of believers moves together. The historical record shows that this process itself produces its own internal disagreements, and the history of the Church comprises a perpetual joining and falling away of adherents. It is the way of things: humans are fallible, even if the truths which are in their custody are not. The historical record also shows that the great miracle of the Faith is that a core of believers has always remained loyal and undivided. Instead of being diverted by the passing sensations of the times, the wise aspirant to truth will seek to join them.